SPIRIT
OF
SURVIVAL

SPIRIT
OF
SURVIVAL

*A Natural and Personal
History of Terns*

JOHN HAY

A Sunrise Book

E. P. DUTTON & CO., INC. | NEW YORK | 1974

Library of Congress Cataloging in Publication Data
Hay, John, 1915–
    Spirit of survival.
    (A Sunrise book)
    Includes bibliographical references.
    1.   Terns.   I.   Title.
QL696.C46H39   598.3'3   73–20402

Published simultaneously in Canada by Clarke, Irwin & Company
Limited, Toronto and Vancouver

ISBN: 0-87690-116-X

Outerbridge and Lazard, a subsidiary of E. P. Dutton & Co., Inc.
Designed by Dorothea von Elbe

In memory of Clarence Leonard Hay

Contents

Acknowledgments ix

CHAPTER 1: *The Eggs* 1

CHAPTER 2: *Travelers* 13

CHAPTER 3: *The Round World* 22

CHAPTER 4: *Voices and Names* 33

CHAPTER 5: *The Magnet of Spring* 41

CHAPTER 6: *Ritual* 52

CHAPTER 7: *A Central Place* 74

CHAPTER 8: *Communication* 90

CHAPTER 9: *Eggs and Their Defenders* 96

CHAPTER 10: *Basic Skill* 107

CHAPTER 11: *Hunger* 118

CHAPTER 12: *Vulnerability* 134

Contents

CHAPTER 13: *Merciless Renewal* 148

CHAPTER 14: *The End of a Season* 157

CHAPTER 15: *Rare as a Tern* 170

Illustrations follow page 82

Acknowledgments

I am indebted to a number of individuals who were kind enough to help me overcome my lack of knowledge on the subject of terns, in particular, Helen Hays, director of the Great Gull Island Program. Both Ian Nisbet and William S. Drury of the Research Department of the Massachusetts Audubon Society were very patient in answering my questions, and I am grateful to them for taking the time to read parts of the manuscript with a critical eye, especially in matters of biology. I also thank Sigurd A. Bruhn of the Zoological Museum at Copenhagen for his hospitable introduction to the terns of Denmark, as well as W. R. P. Bourne of the University of Aberdeen, who guided me toward some of the terneries in Great Britain. I recognize my lack of professionalism in a field that has been carefully studied, notably by Dr. Oliver L. Austin and his son, Oliver L. Austin, Jr., who wrote many papers on the terns they had observed for years in Massachusetts, particularly the colony at Tern Island in Chatham.

Thanks also go to my wife, Kristi, and my daughter, Mrs. Franklin G. Burroughs, Jr., for their help in typing, a job that is lengthy and indispensable. And I appreciated having an editor, John Macrae III, President of E. P. Dutton, who could survive many corrections, rewritings and delays with scarcely a murmur. As far as the book itself is concerned, I only hope I have been able to convey the dimensions of the subject and some of the fascination I found in it.

This book is dedicated to people everywhere who are trying to narrow the gap between man and nature, through self-understanding, and the inclusion of life, "wild, wherever it is."

SPIRIT
OF
SURVIVAL

1

The Eggs

A pair of eggs, tiny, not more than one and a quarter inches long, suddenly materializing in the sand: I had walked by them a number of times before I saw them and could easily have crushed them underfoot without knowing it. They were at Popham Beach in Maine, just above the flood-tide mark with its blackened, stringy weeds, logs that had been rafted in by storms, and bits of tawny or cloudy-gray driftwood. The swinging tidewaters ran offshore, swirling around the great rocks, carrying sea mists speared by sunlight, and behind me, not too far away, were the supermarkets, the new developments, and the asphalted highway taking its preoccupied traffic ten miles or a thousand.

What is more common than an egg? Yet these beige colored, lightly speckled, shiny spheres, only a little larger than pebbles, seemed uncommonly rare. My eyes found them, a wonderfully delicate presence among the sand grains, but when I looked away I lost them again. They were marked like the granular dots, specks, and accents everywhere around them, distinctive and at the same time made to disappear from sight.

Here was a semi-desert by an open sea, under an open sky, with two nearly invisible eggs placed almost accidentally in nothing more than a bare scrape: it seemed to imply a lasting trust in the face of all finality. The fact was that Least Terns would sometimes lay their eggs so close to the tideline that spring tides washed them away, and if that happened early they would lay another clutch in nearly the same place. This sounds fairly stupid, but such a close and confident relationship between being and place must have an element of wisdom in it. Their habits have worked well enough, on balance, to keep the race alive; to think of them only in terms of adaptability might not be wise enough on our part.

Lives that fit the natural scheme take continual loss. Eggs and chicks can be washed away, or killed by exposure if the adults fail to brood them, or eaten by predators. But the Least Terns, tiny and yellow-billed, with a white patch on their foreheads, are fiercely protective. Farther down the beach I saw one chasing a Herring Gull which had evidently come too close to the nest. It seemed like an uneven contest in terms of size, but the little tern went right after the gull and managed to pluck off a white feather, which eddied gently toward the ground. The parents of eggs or chicks can't destroy the "evil" in the sky, but they do their best.

So I found that one wild bird's egg, shaped like the globe itself, lying out in open territory, was a sign of the supreme risk in which all life engages.

During the past twenty-five years and more, the space around me in coastal New England has begun to be so populated, scraped and smoothed over, that in many areas it is no longer recognizable. The birds go on laying their eggs to insure their future on as many open beaches, or marshlands, in such fields, thickets, or woodlands, as they can still find. Some are a good deal more adaptable than others, trying their luck alongside the human race. Others manage less well. More and more, the migratory species literally seem like visitors from foreign lands, and the rest are part of occupied territory. Not that we do not give them some recognition in our way, but our way is the dominant one and lays down the rules of occupation. The natives, we seem to say, are recognized when they are useful to us and not harmful. We bring a certain detachment with us, the result of a lack of working acquaintance with nature, wherever we move in.

On Cape Cod, where I live, the Least Terns have been dispossessed in many areas. Having made a comeback after a terrible decline in population at the end of the nineteenth century, they appear to be going down in numbers again. All the same, this scrappy bird holds its own and returns each year to claim the places it inherited.

The summer I saw the Least Terns in Maine, I also saw two of their nests on a crowded beach on the Cape. The eggs, in little bare scoops in the sand, were surrounded by stones that some would-be protector had put there. Beach-buggy tracks were only yards away and the massed marks of human feet much closer than that. A week later, the beleaguered nests had disappeared.

I had seen other, larger species of terns flying along the shore for a long time and admired their flight. I had taken their presence for granted. Their crying and diving in shallow waters were part of the summer scene and my associations with it, but I knew very little about them aside from that.

"Chock!" With angled wings, the gray and white, black-capped spick-and-span sea bird struck the surface of the tidal waters like an arrow and then rose again with a little fish in its bill carried crosswise. As it flew on with deep and deliberate strokes, its wings seemed to lead to other shores I had never seen.

For years I had thought of giving the terns a closer look. Since they are great travelers, and worldwide in distribution, I could not expect to follow them as far as I should have liked, but I knew of at least one nesting island only about seven miles from where I lived. I had never been there, but heard that this was the breeding place for a sizeable population of Common and Roseate Terns during the summer months. The island turned out to be little more than a sand spit, a stretch of low dunes and hollows surrounded by water at high tide, that constituted the outer boundaries of a salt marsh. I walked out across the wide marsh at low tide, one September day, while the wind whipped up pools and watery aisles and avenues stretching over the sands in the tidal flats beyond.

Tide marshes are places that are sheltered by offshore sandbars or barrier beaches, and take advantage of the curves and indentations in the shoreline. The winds blow freely across them, and their tough, salt-resistant grasses seem to hold the year in place. Channels or streams take the tidewaters through, and then they fill and spread over the levels of the marsh, trickling through, resting and withdrawing. A salt marsh seems to hold tremendous patience, plentiful hours; its life embodies the rhythm of the tides.

On the way out I passed a young Great Black-backed Gull that stood erect not far from me but did not fly away, and I wondered about it. The island, when I reached it, had very little evidence of terns. I found a few scrapes, hardly bigger than my cupped hand, where the birds had had nests between the beach grasses, and I found the delicate, nearly lighter-than-air skull of a tern, dully polished like a white pebble, with a faintly oily sheen.

Still there were a few terns standing inshore on peaty banks and I guessed that some of these were young ones, fully feathered out, but making importunate begging cries. I could see adults bringing fish to them. Water currents shifted in the sunlight, and I heard the "Wheep, wheep" of a startled shorebird. In the distance, the terns uplifted and drew down across the water again, and I felt in me all the tugs of water and wind and the long, long pressure of change in that smoky sky. September was beginning to pull away.

The slender, sharp blades of the beach grass, though green and shiny still, were beginning to have a bleached look. As I walked back toward a tidal creek I had to wade through to reach the shore, the dense "salt hay" grass lay in waved swales where it had been bent over, its stalks still partly green, partly a pinky brown. Farther on, other marsh grasses and reeds bowed their straw-colored seed heads. Plants flattened and sprang up again under my tread, or stiffly rustled, as incoming tidewaters began to trickle around their stems.

When I came back to where I had seen the gull standing, large and handsome, but without much animation, I found it lying dead in the marsh. I had not been away for more than three quarters of an hour. I had no idea what was the matter with it, since it had no marks on it that I could find. It was a strange dying, standing up, unattended, unregarded.

A few adult terns were flying over the waters of the creek where it wound in through the marsh, and near it I also saw a tern that seemed unable to fly away. I had heard that juveniles, before they can really feed themselves, occasionally die for lack of nutrition. Their parents may fail to feed them for some reason, or there may be a lack of fish in surrounding waters. Perhaps, now and then, a Black-back, a nearly omnivorous feeder, will die from what it eats, whereas a selective feeder like a tern will starve. I had no proof of anything, except that the tern, when I ran after it and caught it, had very thin breast muscles.

The bird struggled only feebly as I held it; it was very weak. The long, sharply pointed bill opened in protest, showing a pinkish orange gape and a slender tongue. The pure white feathers on its breast were soft and dense, and the gray of its wings might have come from the lining of a passing cloud. The forked tail expanded and contracted, still taut and willowy in spite of weakness. I knew that this feathered marvel could fly superbly, travel great distances with ease, and live, with luck, for twenty-five years or more. I knew that it was made for all the conjurations of air, the infinite changes in the atmosphere; and at the same time I did not know it at all. The large black eyes bulged a little on both sides of the head, but expressed no weakness that I could recognize. I brought it home and tried to force feed it with minnows, but it was dead by morning.

I do not know that you can come any closer to a bird's essential nature by holding it in your hand, or even by keeping it close at hand for a while. By definition, a wild bird caged or trapped will deceive you as to its nature; its reality lies in freedom. Those uncompassionate eyes tell you very little in any case. All I could sense in that captured tern was a quickness of nerve and heart, and, perhaps, a fear that might have some alliance with my own.

I have heard some off-the-cuff statistics about the relative mental power of men and birds, or for that matter, of men and seals, or men and elephants, but I doubt them. We have a way of measuring the intelligence of other animals in terms of how much they respond, if at all, to our own, so such analogies are likely to have a dubious validity. As to birds, I suppose it is possible to rationalize the difference by saying that they lack our ability to make new forms out of patterns reconstructed from the past and also to project them into the future. But to say they lack memory and foresight is still judging them by our dimensions; their state of being has its own inherited mysteries.

Birds do seem dependent on their immediate inner feelings, which are directly related to the external world and its physical events. They spring rhythmically into action, like the shoals of minnows the Sooty Terns of tropical waters pick up as they skip and flash across the surface. They fly off, scream, stand silently, alight, migrate in response to one another, to wind and sunlight, heat and cold, depths and shallows. They are spontaneous rather than reflective; but there is a high seriousness in them that eludes any relative value judgments we can make.

I had read about their specialized behavior. I had read about those small brains, about their flying skills, their keen eyesight. They had been well annotated and described. Still, something was left unsaid. Perhaps the mere biology of a bird, whose temperature—depending on the species— can be as high as 110 degrees Fahrenheit, and whose heart beat is much more rapid than our own, took it out of our range in the first place. That metabolism seemed too quick for human comprehension. What kind of time-shedding, or time-ignoring, might birds experience? Did we experience our surroundings at a much slower pace, or were we further removed from them simply because of special abilities? I could not understand what it might mean to go through existence at their tempo. Creation offered extraordinary depths and modes of feeling and receptiveness, most of which flew by me unrecognized. Still, if I was not going to get inside the head of a tern, I would at least let it lead me on.

During those warm days in the autumn, when swimming was still good in Cape Cod Bay, I noticed young terns trimly perched on rocks, or on dories moored just offshore. When I was in the water, I could usually get much closer to them than I could on land. But by late summer or early fall many immature terns have not yet acquired a healthy fear of man. I walked up behind and to the side of one of these where it stood on a breakwater with a tiny fish still flipping in its bill, and watched as the bird gradually worked the mouthful down until it disappeared with a final faint motion of the tail. All the while, the single eye that faced me seemed oblivious to me as a threat, to the extent that I wondered at first whether the bird might not be blind in that eye.

So, through September and October, I kept watching the terns for as long as they fished offshore, without precisely knowing what their actions told me, but their buoyant flight, their incessant beating back and forth across the tides, was enough to keep anyone's sight alive.

One day there was a great storm on the Cape. It was not quite of hurricane force; there were no wild, blasting winds to pull the guts out of the place, yanking violently at the trees, as often happens. Though the wind was strong, it was the following rain that seemed to be the major force.

All afternoon it came down intermittently, overwhelmingly. The raindrops were huge; when I walked down to the shore, they were belting and pitting the sands. The marsh grasses and the beach smelled strongly of salt water. When the rain bucketed down from the skies it soaked me through and through, and so quickly that I shivered all over, even though the air was fairly warm.

Out on a sandbar at the mouth of the creek, a number of terns were rising up, curving off in a flock for a short distance and then returning, held down by the rain. I counted nearly forty where they stood on the sands facing into the storm, each one in place. Then a smaller group flew in low behind them, expertly wheeling in and stopping, each individual taking a place with relation to the others that almost seemed prearranged. As they landed they either stood like miniature statues, coming into position immediately, or pattered ahead a little before they stopped. Their disciplined adjustment to the storm was fascinating to watch. They showed a sort of rhythmic tribal placement, practiced in the face of all the odds, the natural disasters, the cosmic standards they had to meet. A tribe with that kind of relationship to the elements, attuned and at the same time in rapt conflict, encouraged exploration in a man who was none too happy with being told that the only relevant order was the human one. They led me forward.

The synchronization of the weather is in me too. My senses inherit it. I am at home in wintertime when the Brant Geese run off low over the shoal lines like great bees, and where the stars on clear nights dive into the tides. Before a coming storm I stand under growing fans of curdled clouds, the change in air against my ears. Migration and constancy belong to the shore, where the gulls are belling and choking, swimming on an apex of light, turning on ripples, electric waters, and running time.

So the terns, with their pliant, airy flight, floated and raced through the process of autumnal change, gray-winged birds, hunting silver fish, moving over the gray Atlantic. They cried "Keearrh!" in the distance, urgently, excitedly. As more and more of them departed, their local numbers dropped, and the small flocks still fishing offshore seemed to tell us distance-trappers to move out of our self-containment.

As often happens in mid-fall, a day swept in when there was nothing less than an upheaval in the atmosphere, bringing a great shift in the wind, an all-immersing blow out of the north. The sea was seared on the horizon. Riled-up waters moved sullenly under gray, rimy clouds, and toward the east hung dark and heavy curtains with streamers running down from them toward the sea. It was as if everything, from the land out across the water, reacted unexpectedly, suddenly, either with reluctant abandon or sullen retreat, under a new will imposed by the Arctic.

The wind blew hard, keeping the water birds low but in the air. There were great flocks and lines of them flying about, storm-crowded close to the shore, beating back and forth over the waves, then dropping down. Geese labored up; Black Ducks hurtled away downwind; shearwaters, usually to be found much farther out, ran cleanly by; gannets with their great winged wheels and pitches down into the sea defied the violence of the air, while just off the beaches the lighter-bodied terns were hovering, casting down along the wind and beating back up again.

Travel filled the coastline. The fall is like that. All kinds of conjunctions and influences come to bear, which can be lengthily described in terms of cyclonic disturbances, local climatic influences, migratory paths (north to south, east to west), the fledging of birds, the dying down of plants, the temperature of water and air, but overwhelmingly present in all feeling things must be that great turn and change, that sending on. Place was life and life was hunger, all the way around the world.

The terns I watched as they beat from side to side across the water seemed to be looking not only for their food but also for the way on. They had a readiness in them to meet and join what lay ahead, for the immediate distance or thousands of miles. Flocks fishing for the still fairly plentiful small fish along the shore were diving and striking into surface waters beyond the beaches. They seemed flexible in a way their marine surroundings enabled them to be, giving them food, shifting or withholding it. I thought the means to face the menace and unpredictability of nature was in them too. They seemed to act with vital fear, plummeting, rising instantaneously, constantly alert between sea and sky, responding to autumnal shifts and relocations. But they were long-distance migrants, with another continent inside them. Many left long before the food supply dwindled with colder weather. Why? What called them, out of what depths? What was the force that made them leave? I never expected to be able to answer the question, but, after all, men have never stopped trying, and have never quite succeeded. Perhaps it is wonder, as usual, that provides the start, if no solution.

I watched the last tern flocks of autumn easily drifting over the near edge of sandbars where the water deepened a mile or so offshore, compensating in flight for the puffs and eddies of the air, their floating ongoingness interrupted by a lifting and dropping down that seemed in outline or profile like the outlines of the waves themselves. Their gray and white bodies over the sea surface made a parallel with the whitecaps on the waves. Reflecting the sunlight as they drifted on, at the same time in fast measure racing and returning, they were like brilliant shards and splinters, slivers and shreds of light.

Miles out over open water, and hard to see now through my fieldglasses, a much bigger flock seemed to turn and hover in mid-air. Then it moved on in a cloud that streamed out and gathered in again, a mass shifting in the full light of the sun, alternately showing white of breast and darker gray of wing. The flock swung off horizontally, spreading and gathering as it went, in a hazy distance, until it finally disappeared.

2
Travelers

The terns had gone away, and the sandy shores had lost a compelling cry. I wondered, in the chilly month of November, how they were distributed on their wintering grounds. They had traveled great distances. Common Terns leaving northeastern America in the autumn months fly south as far as Cape Hatteras and then travel out directly over open water until they reach the Bahamas or eastern Cuba. From there they fly through the West Indies to wintering grounds south of Trinidad, along the eastern coast of South America, from the Amazon Delta as far as Rio de Janeiro.

In recent years it has been discovered that a large part of the Roseate Tern population nesting along New England shores spends the winter off Guyana. (Roseate Terns look very much like Commons, with gray wings, forked tails, and black caps, except that their tails are considerably longer, their wings shorter, their bills black instead of red during the breeding season, and their feathers are a paler, more silvery gray overall.)

So off those lithe riders went into their long miles, over the heavy roll, into the wind drag and the spume, the changing light in those overwater heights that an almost unending past had taught them to know. They had flown nearly halfway across the world, but it was their home. By comparison, to what degree had men lost their ties to locality? Technological achievement is deceiving. We are inclined, in an age of instant communication, to say that it is a globe made small by man; but after the curtains fell on the horizon and the last flock disappeared, I wondered if the terns were not using the earth's resources more directly, more closely, and on a wider scale than we were. Distance was something they could not avoid by surpassing it.

Some say, for want of a better than contemporary reference, that birds are machines, all 9,000 species with their wings, their large hearts, hollow bones, elastic skeletons, and feathers superbly fashioned for insulation, aerial maneuver, and display. And each of these winged creatures, by comparison with ground-dwelling mammals like ourselves, uniquely overcoming clumsiness with mind, is equipped to move spontaneously through the atmosphere so as to find the food and shelter it needs to maintain itself.

Still, a bird is of the air. Can mechanical terms even begin to convey that association of being and atmosphere? Terms such as aerofoils, aspect ratio, or lift and drag only describe a function. Where is sensate flight described? (During my lifetime I have had recurrent dreams of flying, in which I levitated across the room above the heads of a bemused company. What did it mean: aspiration, another try at freedom, an effort to escape from constraint? Perhaps some such unconscious impulse produced the airplane.)

Sea birds, varying greatly in the distances they migrate,

depend on oceanic resources and on breeding territories they can return to around the rims of the globe. Their relation to marine resources and conditions—the plankton, the fish, the radiation of light on shallow or surface waters, the ocean currents, the length of day and night, and the seasonal temperatures—is apparently a matter of recurring action, tried behavior fitted to the specific, if changing, nature of the environment. All this makes the terns a little more fixed than they seemed while I watched them search for fish in Cape Cod Bay. Certainly, the tremendous distances many sea birds, notably the Arctic Tern, undertake, put them in a class that almost goes beyond the conditions they are subject to. As Donald Griffin puts it in *Bird Migration:* "The maximum extent of bird migrations is limited not by the capabilities of the birds, but by the size of the planet."

Of course our special ability to lose, chase, get rid of time, and even to extend ourselves beyond this spinning planet, could take me to the coasts of Europe and Africa, to the Pacific, the Arctic and the Antarctic, or the coast of South America. The terns got there too, but at a more supple pace. Skipping like a demon dragonfly over a lily pond at six hundred miles an hour or more, forty thousand feet in the air, any one of us may be able to circumscribe or even leave the globe. Still, given enough of this time-transcending, I question whether we will be able to relate and to equate ourselves any longer with the ground. We fly above the kind of earth-discovery that used to be unavoidable and had to be contended with.

Where was I, on one of my coastal trips by plane between Boston and New York? Away above tern country certainly. I looked down and occasionally saw gulls and terns flying white and loose over the water, but saving time and challenging gravity brought me no closer than that. Even with the most precise instruments, do we know where we are? From some exterior, I land with a certain lack of continuity, not quite sure of what to do with myself, having passed all miles so soon. I am still a walker, but one who is not well enough attached to his own soil. Is it two thousand walking miles to the Gulf of Mexico? I may never know.

Still, as I stood on the shore again looking out after the unseen terns, there was a remnant wonder in me that smelled the salt marshes and the sea, watched the waves rolling and walking in, and felt those far sea ends where water birds rode with such apparent ease.

I found that Arctic Terns, Wilson's Petrels, Greater Shearwaters, or Long-tailed Jaegers that travel off North America down to South America can be traced to some extent through sightings, and because they return to known breeding areas where they can be banded. Aside from that, their movements become almost impossible to trace with any degree of accuracy. They simply disappear, as far as men are concerned, into the oceans of the southern hemisphere. It is not strange that human longing should have attached itself to birds.

The Arctic Terns are the most fabulous travelers of them all. They nest in temperate regions as well, but their Arctic range extends across northern Alaska and Canada, Greenland, Iceland, northern Europe and Asia. Their nesting season is short—it has to be, to permit such travel—and after it they fly down two main migratory routes, one along the continental shelf of western Europe, passing the coast of Africa, and the other down the Pacific coasts of North and South America, both ending in the southern hemisphere. A certain number of Arctic Terns winter off

South Africa and southern South America, but the majority appear to fly as far as the rim of the Antarctic pack ice, where they spend the winter resting on ice floes and feeding in the leads and openings between them.

An Arctic Tern that nests in north-central Canada and then travels over to Europe, thence south to the Antarctic, makes a journey of some 12,000 miles by the time it reaches its destination. These terns apparently see more daylight than any other birds in the world because of a breeding habit that takes them to northern latitudes where the sun sets late or hardly at all, and a journey to wintering grounds where there are only short hours of darkness.

On the autumn migration, Arctic Terns crossing the Atlantic are probably helped by favorable winds. Then they evidently travel down the coasts of Europe and Africa in a fairly deliberate way, feeding as they go. When they reach South Africa they have largely used up their physical resources and their wing feathers are frayed and weakened; while the journey ahead of them, across several hundred miles of stormy seas to the Atlantic, is the hardest yet. Still, it is supposed that they travel fast on their final lap, resting only briefly on scattered icebergs and occasional islands along the way. This is a region of strong winds and heavy gales, but the flight of terns is bending and flexible, and they are evidently able to ride the winds and keep their general direction.

It is hard to believe, when first looking at an Arctic or Common Tern, that either of them is capable of making such journeys. Both species seem to have a loose, almost erratic flight against a strong wind. But their wings, at the same time, have a sure and tireless beat. When I saw a dead tern stripped of its feathers for mounting, I was chiefly impressed by two things: the large size of the eye cavity, not uncommon in birds, and the strength of the shoulder muscles.

On the Maine coast, toward the end of the summer and just after a minor hurricane, I watched some Common Terns flying over stormy seas just off Pemmaquid Point. They were in hurried and at the same time twisting, bending flight, their long, pointed wings like thin, angled leaves tossed in a gale. The wind was blowing at forty or fifty miles an hour, and they would go down into the troughs of the waves to escape it and then lift again, making slow forward progress. The sea surface was full of green waves like a range of hills. Rocks, sea, and sky all glittered with the high glory of light a hurricane leaves behind it, while the surf boiled under the sun, roaring and rushing in, a massive amalgam of white and silver against the rocky shore.

One thinks of fluidity, migratory waves, and dispersals in connection with some birds such as petrels which spread out over great areas on migration. Others, like the terns, seem more closely knit, whether in small groups or large flocks. But both return consistently to their breeding areas, and have to be credited with built-in discipline and a remarkable sense of direction. That such small birds should be able to weigh all seas in the balance of their travels, gauging hundreds of miles as if they were yards, gives them a degree of ability for which our own senses seem to have no equivalent.

I also found out that Sooty Terns, fledged in the Dry Tortugas off southern Florida, migrated in their first autumn all the way across the tropical Atlantic to the Gulf of Guinea. Only the young seemed to make such a migration. The adults left their breeding grounds after nesting, but appeared to go no farther than the neighboring Gulf of

Mexico and the Caribbean. The route these juveniles took was apparently twenty percent longer than a direct line traced across the Atlantic would have been. The reason they did not take a more direct route was that the longer one presented them with less resistance from storms and prevailing winds.

W. B. Robertson* has this to say to those who can trace the birds either in their mind's eye or on a map:

> The migrants cross the tropical cyclone belt of the Atlantic by the southerly leg of the route in the western Caribbean and make their easting in the nearly storm-free area of the extreme southern Caribbean. Hurricanes are the chief known cause of the death of fledged Sooty Terns, and intersecting storms in August and September, 1901–1967, were twice as frequent (154 compared with 78) along the direct route compared with the route we believe the terns follow. A southeasterly tack along the Guyanan coast carries migrants across the northeast trade wind belt and enables them to complete their Atlantic crossing in the light winds and calms of the intertropical convergence. Approaching Africa on this course should at times encounter favorable winds of the onshore monsoon. Because most of the flight is opposite to the prevailing direction of surface winds and storm movement, a route that voids or minimizes the hazards of areas of more frequent hurricanes and stronger contrary winds may be particularly significant for survival. Prevailing winds doubtless assist the return flight, the most favorable conditions probably occurring in February and March when the northeast trade winds extend farthest south.

* W. B. Robertson, "Transatlantic Migration of Juvenile Sooty Terns," *Nature*, vol. 223, no. 56182 (May 1969), pp. 632–634.

Having dabbled that much in other men's findings, quickly tracing these phenomenal routes over the globe, behind the terns, behind their ancient use of the seas in understanding, I could see that bird study was a study of magnitude. If birds failed to extend our distances, the problem must not be with them but the world of their beholders.

Of course there are summations we can make about migration. There are biological factors and environmental conditions that make a sea bird very much a part of the marine world whose ranges it seeks out for its food. Birds not only use the great prairies of the oceans, they are habituated to them, and each species has its own way of ordering its numbers with respect to the food they provide, and learning its own directions.

The Arctic Tern, spontaneously flying off over thousands of miles of ocean, leaves a nesting area at a time when its food supply is giving out, and, in extraordinary style, heads for another pole to find it. Migration aids in the geographical distribution of birds, and since the earth's own habits stay rhythmically the same for great periods of time, these creatures with ages of habit in them respond partly in terms of heredity. Evolution has apparently geared their genetics so that terns respond to appropriate conditions on a continental, or in the case of the Arctic species, on a global scale. Countless years of climatic cycles have been impressed on the normal rhythm of their lives. Their sexual cycle, their ways of feeding, and their movements from one area to another have so evolved that their young hatch out where there is a periodic abundance of food, and their populations are distributed to best advantage.

Nevertheless I was about as far from reaching scientific

interpretations and conclusions as I was from genuine knowledge of the birds themselves. All we had was a common earth. That is why I went out occasionally at night when wind and clouds separated from one another and the stars shone out in caves between the uplifted arms of the trees, to do a little wandering, imagining the migrant terns plying their seas. I felt I might come a little closer to them as they beat down the southern coasts, or flew over blue water, in and out of storms, or making fair and free way beyond them, on lags, on various jags of travel, avoiding the worst or sometimes meeting it, dropping and bending from side to side, with their long wings, against a heavy wind, bounding swiftly ahead with air currents that were easy for them, until finally they reached a farther coast which their young may never have seen before but at the same time knew, a reach that had some fine inner justice to it which I imagine we too sense and hope for from time to time.

The charts we used for other lives and distances never seemed to me to quite catch up with those flyers using the present a little beyond our range, although we hardly ever admitted this. Since we pretended to control the difficulties of nature, if not of our personal lives, in taming hurricanes, avoiding uncharted travel, building up the Gross National Product so that it would somehow take care of most wanderings from our course, we might well think of these small-brained birds as helpless. Why throw yourself into the teeth of an icy gale if you don't have to? The discipline in a bird that counted on all earth and its inheritance as being open to it finally escaped us. I envied its constancy.

3

The Round World

A hunk of ice in the creek nudged another one and then cracked in half. As far as I could see, from my eye level on the beach, ice cakes were floating out on the bay. In the Arctic, I understand, the ice groans, shrieks, and thunders, enough to give a frightened soul a turn for the worse, but here the temporary pack ice rafted up on the beach; the slush in semi-frozen sea water, gently rotated by the tides, hardly seemed ominous.

Though the terns were gone, the Herring Gulls, their near relatives, were crowding the local dumps, and down by the shore with gray and white wings, soft under softly clouded skies, they accepted the new ground on the water, flying smoothly over it and then landing. There are gulls and terns around the world, taken for granted in most local areas where men see them, but varying subtly in their needs and manner in whatever latitude they are found. (Lately the gulls, omnivorous scavengers, ready and capable of taking advantage of new food resources, have been managing much better by human presence than the terns.)

It was hard to believe that the island in the salt marsh where the terns had nested had ever been loud with their cries, its days and nights made intense by them, filled with waves of excitement and alarm. The marsh grasses lay flattened, some of them like coarse animal hairs, and the cold wind whistled over them. Now that the beach grasses and other plants had died down, the sandy dips and hollows of the nesting island itself seemed even more exposed, and the strip of beach in front of it lay narrow and hard under icy blades of air.

I saw a Great Blue Heron rising up out of the marsh, with big bowed wings, then settling slowly farther on, to disappear finally into the confines of a ditch. I wondered how much of its preferred food was left. A winter that ices over the streams and freezes the marsh too hard and for too long a time is deadly for a heron. There was hunger in the salt marsh, and in the thickets and woodlands behind it, a general hunger in the midst of crisis. Rabbits or mice crouched there, wary of hawks and owls, wary of a great many dangers. Every dash of cold or swell of warmth in the wind impinged on their senses. Every change from melting snow to ice to snow again, or to rain, affected the food on which they nibbled. Where they slept, or jumped in fear, where—if they lived that long—they would feel spring anger and desire, was a place of tactile sensations in them and other lives, awake to all influences, the weather as much as any. Each cloud that passed could be significant.

(Our own winter seemed to be full of enormous seizures suddenly overcoming one part of the globe, while in another there were painful contractions or ominous expansions. At the same time, very few local people could tell you about real weather, the kind whose strictures were well known to a heron or a field mouse. Did we imagine we could get along without it?)

Wintry, naked, and wild, the tern's island was still patiently waiting, as all other such places were, for the occupation that spring would make possible again. What brings terns back and ties them down to nesting territories? A recurring food supply, we say, as well as inherited directions, habit, biological change, the distributory needs of the globe; but is it not also the force of those places with which the birds have lasting, reciprocal relationships? This island they used was in itself a living entity, made up of innumerable parts, animate and inanimate; it followed the laws that attracted a fury of life in spring and summer and kept it latent during winter's hunger, laws that were applicable over the face of the earth, measurable in human terms, nearly immeasurable in its diversity. A half-acre of land that we value in dollars and human possession, and dispose of accordingly, was not only a definite point of reference but had awe-inspiring reach.

So this limited territory, littered on its rim with tidal wrack, its beach grasses gone straw-yellow with a chewed and ragged look at the butt like old cornstalks, was, on balance, as receptive to growth as countless such places from pole to pole. The terns, along with other colonially nesting birds such as gannets, auks, and kittiwakes, have magnetic ties to sand and rock, to the configurations of plants, the motion in offshore waters. They have a style that attaches and in a sense identifies.

Once I saw only a gull, then both gulls and terns. After that I began to notice the differences among species of gulls and terns. That kind of practice, for all the futility we may find in mere naming, was more revealing than I had imagined. It began to free my sight of some of its bounds, because each new kind seemed to lead to a new country, a way of life I had never met with before. So to read that terns comprise some thirty-nine species is now more to me than a figure on a page.

Not all the terns are confined strictly to salt water, nesting on sandy or rocky shores. A number of species nest in both salt- and freshwater marshes, and sometimes, as in the case of the Black Tern, in shallow inland ponds or lakes with a growth of reeds along their edges. The Common Tern ranges widely over inland lakes as well as the seacoast. Other terns are native to rivers in various parts of the world. All of them have a similar way of fishing, hovering over the surface with beak pointed downward before they dive; and most have a bouncy, deliberately stroking kind of flight. They are long-winged, slender birds as compared with gulls. They are fairly shallow divers and are generally thin-plumaged, with a relative absence of underdown. Unlike birds such as cormorants and members of the auk family which can pursue fish underwater, they are poor swimmers and cannot stand prolonged immersion.

Most of them have similarly harsh cries, though the Peruvian Tern, locally called "Churi-Churi," is said to have a sweet, musical note, more like a shore bird's than a tern's. Many have forked tails, though some, like the Common, Arctic, Roseate, and Royal Terns, have tails that are more deeply indented than others, with long outer tail feathers called "streamers." For this reason they have been called "sea swallows," especially those of the black-capped, gray-winged variety, though their flight is not precisely swallow-like, having a steady, buoyant beat of its own, without the sailing, checking, twisting maneuverability of the shorter-winged swallow as it chases insects in the air. I have seen Common Terns catch flying ants high over a Maine cove with considerable skill, but their ability to turn as swallows do is limited by the greater length of their wings.

The association of terns with swallows may not be entirely a matter of forked tails. The Black Tern has a tail that is only slightly forked, but as it sweeps across inland marshes catching insects, it reminds me of a swallow more than other species do. (And, if only to indicate how functions overlap in nature, regardless of species, there is the Pratincole, or Swallow-Plover, of Europe, Africa and Asia, an insect-eater with long pointed wings and a forked tail. It is called a plover because it runs like one.)

The largest tern, the Caspian, is about the size of a Ring-billed Gull. The Royal Tern is another relatively large species, though less heavy in appearance and flight. The Least Tern, called Little Tern in Europe, is the smallest; a similar bird is the Damara Tern, native of the southwest coast of Africa.

The terns are divided into three genera: *Sterna*, including the black-capped ones, which are in the majority; *Anous*, including the noddies, all found in tropical seas; and *Larosterna*, a monotypic genus comprising the Inca Terns, an ornamental little bird found in the region of the Humboldt Current off the west coast of South America. Inca Terns have slate-gray feathers, a bill that Robert Cushman Murphy, the ornithologist, called "dragon-red," and coral-red feet. They are adorned with a curving white plume on each side of their head, extending from below the eye. They nest in cliffside burrows, an unusual habitat for terns, and in flight they make quick swoops, fluttering and dashing over the surface of the sea, sometimes picking up fish almost out of the jaws of a sea lion as it comes mouthing and snorting to the surface.

"You should have been with us," a lucky traveler said to me one day, "when we were approaching the Marquesas in a boat. There were hundreds of pure white Fairy Terns flying around and around, with nearly translucent feathers with a greenish cast because of the waters reflected from below."

The Fairy Tern, one of the noddies, appears to be one of those successful but at the same time wayward products of an evolution that fulfills special needs but also holds surprise in reverse. It looks almost ethereal, like "tiny flying skeletons" according to Murphy's *Oceanic Birds of South America*, but is at the same time as intense and precise in its ways as most other terns. When I saw one, not in the Pacific but at the Bronx Zoo, it made me think that primal extravagance must always be close by, innate in all normal and expected things. Perhaps there is some "off limits" potential in any life form that is part of the momentum of survival.

The Fairy Tern is found along the South Atlantic as well as the Pacific, breeding on small islands and wooded mainland shores. Sometimes called "White Tern" or "Holy Ghost Bird," it is almost totally white except for its black eyes, which have a black circle around them, making them look like disproportionately large and shining pits. In the brilliant tropical sunlight the bird's light wings and body seem transparent, skeletal, with nothing more to intercept the light than the outline of flesh and bones. These improbable little birds sometimes hover wheezing in the presence of human beings like so many curious insects, close enough to be picked up by hand. They take not one but two or three small fish in their bills at a time, carried crosswise as they fly to feed their chicks.

This tern lays one egg, on a rock or a slightly indented branch, where its balance is in great jeopardy. All the same, eggs and chicks manage not to fall to the ground. I have heard that newcomers to the tropics are often offered bets on how long the egg or chick of a Fairy Tern will remain on its precarious perch, and if they wager on a fall they are bound to lose. The parent bird breeds the egg in a semi-standing position, so as to shade it and keep it at the right temperature, at the same time clinging securely to its perch. The chicks are also equipped with strong claws which enable them to hang upside down by one foot if knocked over, and to swing back up again like acrobats.

The greater number of tern species are to be found in warm waters. There are more in the Pacific than the Atlantic, and those of us who live along northern or temperate coasts are not likely to see more than a few as compared with the tropics. Several million Sooty Terns, dark-winged birds of a more placid disposition than the Arctic or the Common species, breed on one of the Seychelle Islands in the Indian Ocean, and about 100,000 others inhabit the Dry Tortugas off the southern tip of Florida, where they nest on the ground. When John James Audubon, cruising among the Florida Keys in 1832, landed among the Sooty Terns of the Dry Tortugas, he felt that they would "raise me from the ground, so thick were they all around us, and so quick was the motion of their wings. Their cries were deafening."

Another famous colony of Sooty Terns, on Ascension Island in the mid-south Atlantic, is called "Wideawake Fair" because of the constant clamor of its population, night and day. In a scene out of *Oceanic Birds of South*

America that seems approached as through a lens from the sky, its dense populations are described in this way:

> The site is well sheltered from the wind by hills and is very oppressive under the full blaze of the tropical sun, the more so because of an overpowering odor that arises from it during the time that the birds are present. The stench comes not alone from the guano but also from dead bodies of young and adults and innumerable cracked and addled eggs, among which carrion beetles and their larvae swarm. From the slopes of Green Mountain one can see the area as a greenish white patch, looking as though the bed of cinders had been whitened by a light fall of snow, while in the air above the wheeling and hovering terns appear like a pillar of cloud that is never dissipated during the hours of daylight. The tremendous noise, which is so discordant and ear-splitting at close range, blends in the distance to a sound like the murmuring of a vast crowd of human beings.

Where I walked the cold sands in mid-January, I thought of those sea-swept distances, full of the kind of uncompromisingly rich and brutal energies that New England was not only a little scared of but was putting some effort into avoiding. Continental edges and potentials lay before the sea birds. Flocks of terns spread apart and then came together in the shimmering air off the great coast of Africa. They rippled in the light off beaches by the Indian Ocean and scanned the surface of waters all gem blue and milky green, where fishermen in wooden dugouts with lateen sails moved in toward shore. They fluttered loosely in the distance over great inland lakes. Some hawked for insects while others dove in shallow waters for fish. There were African Skimmers, allied to terns, whose strange long protruding mandibles sheared the surface, stirring up small fish. Perhaps there was a flock of them now resting on a sandbar in the Nile. When a boat passed by, or something mildly disturbed them, they rose off the bar and then returned with dexterous strokes of their wings, as if they were patting the air.

Terns are part of the great, ancient breathing and abiding of the African continent. Their rhythmic behavior belongs to the ebb and flow of offshore tides, of grassland and bush, of drought, fire, and flood, of lakes with sodium-encrusted shores, heavy-running rivers, warm, sullen seacoasts, mountains covered with huge and shining leaves. They are involved with miraculous detail the world around. Dipping for fish in tropical lagoons, beating between the ice floes, meeting the variations of water and weather everywhere, the tern wings take the high contrasts of nature in their stride.

The cold waters gulped here and there as they swirled along the banks of the creek. Tidal New England country, between the pressures of north and south, alternately icy and released, waited out the semi-frozen months. Bad weather ran in, with the scattering and spitting of icy rain. Snow slanted across the salt marsh. The sun came out briefly. Breath came slow. Retreat seemed appropriate, but the hunger to counter it was still a force in the outdoor world.

We do not think enough of the freedom and appropriateness of the weather. It surpasses all compartments of the mind. While we try for a uniformity in all seasons it practices unending change.

At low tide, the great air swept wide across the flats under a spreading, scudding fan of clouds. Across the rippled sands I heard a sort of lowing, along with croupy grunts and growls, from Black-backed Gulls, and then a ripping, low screech from a Herring Gull. A small flock of Canada Geese were standing just at the inland edge of the receding tide. They stalked with a dignified, rolling gait, their rear wings and tails switching from side to side.

These sounds, the birds, the fast skies and the silvery waters were everywhere interrelated, yet moved beyond my hearing and my sight. Gulls and geese kept their rhythmic place or lifted it to other lands. I did not have to go too far after all to see travel on a global scale.

But it was a stiff winter day, with plenty of frozen-in reality all around me. Aside from the birds, I could see few travelers except those who were in machines, and some offshore draggers working hard to overcome a drastic decline in the supply of fish. The trials of the sea had become distant from our experience, and in a relatively short time; perhaps we had left them too quickly, and might have to return one day, if the sea would receive us. I thought of those ocean voyages over monotonous and unforgiving waves, the human migrations that were not only rough but often disastrous, and, at the same time, passionately sought out. Though its expectations may have been shorter then, life was no less desirous.

The Anglo-Saxon poem, "The Seafarer," says:

> The man knows not, the prosperous being, what some of those endure who most widely pace the paths of exile. And yet my heart is now restless in my breast, my mind is with the sea-flood over the whale's domain; it fares widely over the face of the earth, comes again to me eager and unsatisfied; the lone-flier screams, resistlessly urges the heart to the whale-way over the stretch of the seas.

The hail flew in showers. I heard naught there save the sea booming, the ice-cold billow, at times the song of the swan. I took my gladness in the cry of the gannet and the sound of the curlew instead of the laughter of men, in the screaming gull instead of the drink of mead. There storms beat upon the rocky cliffs; there the tern with icy feathers answered them.

4

Voices and Names

The word *tern* seems to have originated along the coasts of northern Europe, whose people knew raw weather and had in them the terror and shapes of unknown worlds. For thousands of years, they carried it in their heads whenever an Arctic or a Common Tern cried out with its "Keearr" or "Teearr," and they had a good many other names, now unused, for these and other terns. Before accurate, or at least scientific, distinctions were made between separate species, local naming had a wonderful diversity. There was such a wealth of common names, with varying pronunciations, from county to county, village to village, coast to coast, that it is often nearly impossible to tell where those names came from or what they had specific reference to. I once met Mrs. Edwin Muir, widow of the distinguished poet. She was brought up on an isolated island off the Scottish coast. She spoke to me of oral tradition, the words and stories that come down "in the air," as she put it, transmitted electrically from generation to generation. A lan-

guage and its names had the texture of local life. It came
from a native earth, and sound of offshore waves and wind,
and a distinctive sky.

Years ago, too, I talked with a Maine lobsterman who
did not know what I meant when I referred to terns. He
finally decided that I was speaking of "medricks," which is
what they are called, as well as "mackerel gulls," along that
part of the coast and northward into Canada. The name
suited better in the state of Maine, a little closer to Europe
than any other—Maine with its monumental rocks walking
into the sea, the salt water brimming up through coves and
islands for thousands of miles of intricate coastline, calling
the wings over and the sails. The summer waters were calm
under light surface airs, but with sudden rushes and
splashes through them like the presence of great fish. Cormorants riding the water dipped over and in quickly, with
their backs curving, and the lobsterman's kids did the
Twist outside a gray shack perched on gray rock, storm-
sanctioned, visited by mauve mists and lapped by tides a
lichen-green. Crows of ragged wing drummed out harsh
alarm calls: "Cadah! Cadah!" along the spruce-ranked
shores behind them. When men, women, and children used
speech that evolved with the measures of the earth itself,
their words followed a bird for a thousand years, walked
the seasons, rowed off from the outhauls of the sea to an
anchored, stony beach.

"Medrick," or a word somewhat like it, probably came
from Europe, but there may be other colloquial names for
terns that sprang up after the settlement of the new world.
I found two for the Least Tern, names that fit an attractive
little bird very nicely: it has been called "striking peter" in
Florida, and in some places along the Mississippi and its

many tributaries, where this bird nests on sandbars, its name is "minner hawk."

"Paytrick," which may be allied with "medrick," is commonly used in Newfoundland, as well as "pietrie," and both words may derive from a British folk name, "picka-tiere" or "pickietar." "Piccatarne" and "pictarne," which resemble the Swedish "tärna," were used in the British Isles. An ancient British word *starn*, is evidently the origin of a good many variants and is related to the Swedish *tärna* and Danish *terne*, as well as to the Norwegian *terna*, and the French word *sterne*. The Spanish word is *charran*.

All these names seem to have originated in the cry of the bird, which sounds much the same in the Common and the Arctic species, although the two have some distinctly different calls, and their voices differ in pitch, emphasis, and tone. In Europe, where both terns and swallows are found, there were equivalents of "sea swallow" in French ("hirondelle de Mer"), Italian ("rondine de Mar"), German ("seeschwalbe"), and Dutch ("zeezwalou"). The Welsh name for sea swallow is "gwennol y mor."

In Britain, terns have also been called "sea mews." George and Ann Marples, in their book *Sea Terns or Sea Swallows*, list "kirrmew" as well as "kirmsu"; "kip," which sounds like one of the calls of the Common Tern; and "clett." Other names, whose derivations they could not account for, are "miret," "rittoch," and "rippock," although they too echo the cries of a tern.

Descriptive names include the Danish "havterne" (*hav* means *sea*) for the Arctic Tern. In Swedish the same bird is "silver-tärna" and the Common Tern is known as the fish tern ("fisktärna"). A Common Tern is a "fjordterne" in Danish. In Swedish the name of the big Caspian Tern is "skräntärna," referring to its scream. "Screecher" or "screamer" has been used in the British Isles for several of the tern species. One Scandinavian name is "ysgraell," meaning "rattle," and a Welsh name for the Arctic Tern is "ysgraell Gogledd," or "northern rattle."

Terns, especially the Commons, are also known as mackerel gulls or mackerel terns in parts of the world other than Europe and North America, because they often follow fishing boats and even lead them to the source of supply. The Japanese name for the Common Tern is "ajisashi" or "horse-mackerel tosser"; for the Least Tern it is "ke-aljisashi" or "little horse-mackerel tosser."

In Portugal a tern is a "gaivina" and in the Cape Verde Islands it is "garajau," with a soft *g*. Cross the tern-traveled seas to Brazil, and you will hear the Common Tern called "trinta reis," and in some parts of South America, the name for this and others such as the Royal is "gaviotin."

The tern the North American Eskimo knows best is the Arctic, and here again the cry of the bird is often reflected in the names men give it. Two of these, said to refer to the Arctic Tern's voice, are "tu-kuthl-kwi-uk" and "tiru-yarak." Another dialect name for that species, which sounds to me when pronounced rapidly like the staccato cry of a tern when attacking an intruder, is "ki-ti-ki-tee-ach." The Aleutian Tern, a bird common to Alaska, is called "chuf-chuf-chee-yuk," or "eg-lug-na-guk," a name referring to its white forehead.

I found a reference in *Birds of Alaska** to the Arctic Tern as "mitkotailyak," meaning "drooping feathers," though why this was applied to so neat and trim a bird was not at all clear. But I am indebted to Dr. William S. Drury

---

* Ira N. Gabrielson and Frederick C. Lincoln, *Birds of Alaska* (Wildlife Management Institute. Harrisburg, Pa.: The Stackpole Co., 1959).

of the Massachusetts Audubon Society for a translation that comes a little closer to its characteristics: "The Eskimos at Eclipse Sound said that their name for Arctic Terns (which is the same as Alaskan 'mitkotailyak' and Greenland 'immerquatailaq') means that he walks on his belly, i.e., has very short legs."

To a white man accustomed to precise systems of classification and nomenclature, Indian and Eskimo words for plants and animals might seem vague and inaccurate, but in most cases the opposite is true. Their vocabulary is rich and their names subtle and descriptive. Names for plants and animals often refer to the kind of inconspicuous differences that most white men would not be aware of; they do not classify, they describe, with the kind of detail that reflects a close dependence. Native people were not only observers of what we proudly call "non-human life," they knew themselves as a part of it. They belonged to the same kingdom.

Indian and Eskimo names reflect the characteristics of the living things they refer to, and often suggest a wide range of action. Among the Chippewas, the Powatamis, and the Algonkians, almost uniformly, a bird was a "bineshi," a bird in rapid flight was a "kikisse bineshi," and if it flew low to the ground it was a "tabassisse bineshi." There were also qualifying terms for a small bird as well as a large one, a bird with wings closed, and a bird hatched naked as distinguished from one hatched with feathers. Even a bird starting to fly off had a distinctive name.

The Massachusetts Indians had a word for a single bird, for a number of birds, and for a little bird ("psukses").

I find, incidentally, that the Crees, of Algonkian stock, still occupying large parts of Canada, refer to a tern as "keya'skoos." Unfortunately, since Indian languages were not written down, stemming from oral tradition, a great many other specific names of that kind are now lost to us.

Without writing, scientific specimens, and the abstract relationships we depend on, Indians and Eskimos knew birds extremely well. Individuals, as in all races, might differ in their ability to recognize one species from another, and some languages probably had more names for them than others, but they were able through memory and mutual association to transmit accurate characteristics of birds and consistent knowledge of them from generation to generation.

Their names for birds are often wonderfully descriptive and evocative. Through them, you hear and see the subject. One bird might be identified by its way of calling in flight and another by something distinctive in its appearance.

The Nunamiut Eskimos of the interior of Arctic Alaska called the young of the American Gyrfalcon "atkuarvak," which means "like caribou mittens." The Red-breasted Merganser was "akpaksruayook," or "runs (like a man) on top of water." The Northern Short-eared Owl was "nipailyntak" or "the screecher"; the Baird's Sandpiper was "nuvuksruk," meaning "sounds like a man with a bad cold."*

Then, of course, there was "mitkotailyak" for the short-legged Arctic Tern, or its "drooping feathers," which could conceivably refer to the way the bird's wings hang during courtship. In some of the old Eskimo stories, too, terns had an important part, as interesting, spicy, aggressive characters.

Clearly, these names come from a close world, an inti-

* Laurence Irving, "The Naming of Birds by Nunamiut Eskimo," *Arctic*, vol. 6, no. 1 (March 1953).

macy toward natural environments, which in a great many regions, perhaps most, is being swept away. The overpowering need of civilization is driving out local identity. Eskimos or Indians, once on speaking, hearing, seeing terms with plants and birds, have other distractions. They depend on a power that is alien to their world, their skills, and often their self-respect. When their language goes too, so does their care for nature and their inner knowledge of earth.

The way life was named and passed on had analogies between Europe and America long before we landed on these shores. So an Eskimo living on the Arctic coast might pass on his knowledge of a bird's call or its feathers as a fisherman did who lived on one of the bare and fog-swept islands of the Shetlands or the Orkneys, north of Scotland. We know, in any case, that both heard the "keearr" of an Arctic Tern far more directly than most of us do now.

Civilized speech and the things it names has long since left its remote forest communities and even its islands far behind, though there is a sense in which our breeding cliffs are still with us. Listen at a distance to a contemporary crowd of people and they might sound like the high and at the same time guttural, cacophonous crying of colonies of sea birds. I think of the thousands of gannets I once saw crowded on their high island in the St. Lawrence, sending out a continual groaning and rattling. And I have heard the sound of kittiwakes, the graceful little gulls that nest on the rocky sides of cliffs in Newfoundland, Denmark, Ireland, and Scotland, a mixture of braying and light bugling—"wittyway-wittyway-wittyway"—against a background of heavy seas or swashing tides, accompanied very often by the donkey-like brays of cormorants and a barking and mewing by the larger gulls. In some regions, puffins grunted and purred and murres called out hoarsely but melodically, a soft "ahhrr" that added to the clamorous harmony on their breeding sites. The colonial sea birds, each species with its typical nesting site—burrow, bare rock, or grassy cliff—belong to ancient establishments, out of that unanswerable demand in nature that brings them back, year after year, over thousands of years, to their cities of life.

5

The Magnet of Spring

Over the years, I have come to look for the same events to be renewed: the singing of peepers in the bogs, the arrival of alewives in the brook. I want to feel life, raw as a codfish pulled out of the cold sea, quiet as an ant, clean running as a swallow, deep throated as a Great Black-backed Gull. The world of nature, this extension of life has come to mean a free opening for me into insights I could never have come upon otherwise. I need the "lower forms." I need the frogs, the box turtles, or the chickadees to declare themselves in front of me. I want to experience evidence not yet by-passed by human totality. Now when I know the terns are in the area, or on their way, it is as if a fine tribe had come in offering *me* beads and knives, and not the other way around. I am the one who needs the enlightenment. I need to shift now, not into another gear, but an alliance. When everything else is waking up, why should I remain dormant until I am given other instructions by the economy?

Spring, casting its lives into the open, is a major event,

even a fury. It frees not only the flowers but the demons. Wild rites and casualties come on, and all things are called to participate.

At the bottom of a high-banked, swampy hollow near my house, the chorus of *Hyla Crucifer*, the spring peeper, swells and dies down with a passionate instantaneousness that speaks for three billion years of earth. Once I took the family dog down there after dark, with wind shaking the still leafless trees and moonlight leaking through the clouds. A high-pitched, scratchy warbling rose up as we came near, and then a scattered belling and tinkling, followed by silence; and then another wave of choiring. The dog whimpered, and when we got to the edge of the hollow, began acting wildly. The wind shook the trees and the moon's reflection danced on their trunks and branches and across pools of water, while the hylas bubbled and rang out intermittently on the far side of the hollow. The dog seemed to find it an experience he was unable to sort out, and ran frantically around, stopping, whimpering, and then wildly barking. With our separate endowments, I could find it exalting, and the dog find it hair-raising, but we had both come to primal openings where light and sound are as fierce and fresh as all the senses newly born to meet them.

Something ancient and at the same time radical happens again as the terns, thousands of miles away, begin their flight north, as offshore fish circle and school and move into warmer waters, and the phytoplankton blooms at a peak of abundance in the sea. There are times when we have to join the wild in spite of ourselves, when we are spontaneously drawn in, like the children along the banks of the herring brook who try to catch the slippery alewives swimming inland to spawn. The fish crowd up in the fish ladders. They leap ahead like a pulse. The girls scream and the boys yell whenever they catch one and their wet hands shiver trying to hold it, their whole bodies shiver, as the alewife violently struggles, gasping for air. Nature meets with nature. They scream with that silver fire in their hands because it is strange, and because they cannot let go what is a part of them.

The migratory journey of the terns is faster, more urgent in the spring than in the autumn, but it takes a Common or a Roseate several weeks to fly up the coast and reach its nesting site; so it can be assumed they leave Central and South America in late March or early April. They fly offshore over the continental shelf in their deliberate, flexible way, feeding occasionally as they go, possibly quickening their pace as they approach their nesting territories. They travel by night as well as by day, and, at an average speed that has been estimated to be around thirty miles an hour, they can presumably cover several hundred miles a day without difficulty.

From south to north along the coastline, groups of terns arrive progressively later on their nesting territories. Those returning to a region where they have nested before are likely to return to a specific site. Terns that have successfully bred in one place have a strong compulsion to come back to it, and these birds collect offshore for a while before they stimulate each other to move in.

They are not all consistent, in any given colony, about their time of arrival. Already mated pairs may arrive sooner than two-year-old unmated birds, and there may be a certain amount of searching by individual birds between one island and another in any given region before they settle down.

"Site tenacity" is a term Oliver Austin, Jr., used to describe the tendency of individual birds to return to the same nesting territory. This apparently provides the binding force between terns and their islands, though it is less highly developed in them than in some other birds. Even after a colony has moved in and started their courting and breeding, individuals may switch to another territory. It is always possible too for a whole colony to move out and settle somewhere else, because of predation, the pressure of gulls, rats, lack of food, and other disturbance, but this may not entirely be a matter of extreme emergency. If the move is made early enough in the season, they can still breed successfully, but the element of room is essential. The species counts on leeway, on another base, another outlet in an always shifting environment. They have been able to, for ages past. But if room is refused them, what then?

The main thing, as I walked back to their empty nesting island in the marsh, was that the terns were on their way, or had already arrived, miles offshore. This fact drew me, as the smelt are drawn to the waters of a northern stream, or a flycatcher to the distant nest it occupied the year before. During the winter, one of those rare countrymen who still know their land for its living more than they know how much it is worth as real estate stood by an iced-over cranberry bog and told me what he knew about otters and muskrats. Otters, he said, enjoyed the worst kind of winter weather, sliding on ice or swimming under it, to break it when they needed air by butting up with their heads. He showed me bubbles in the ice where he said muskrats had been. Being an identifiable part of place these days was something original. I felt as if the terns, like him, might fill me in about a great deal of home detail that I would have ignored without them.

I find it frustrating to speculate about long-distance migration and its reasons, perhaps because it is now so difficult to conceive of organic feats. We are too accustomed to mechanical achievements. I have found out a little simply by following alewives or watching birds go away and return. But, for all the theories, I still keep asking: Why? Why does a tern leave the coast of the Antarctic or South America to head for its breeding grounds? Why does an alewife come out of unknown distances at sea and head for the stream it grew up in, a stream that may be no more than a few yards wide? Simply because it knows how, or because it has to? Obviously these won't do as answers, and scientists have to go further and further in tracing the phenomenon from one reasonable or proved hypothesis to another. Theory leads us to achievement; but when all is said and done, or nearly so, I wonder whether the knowing, the time-honored spontaneity in a sea turtle or a salmon, will not remain the ultimate puzzle.

When I began to read some of the literature on bird migration, I realized that there was no use setting down any of the factors casually; but one of the few that consistently influence a bird's biology is the variation in length of days that follows the changing position of the earth in relation to the sun. Longer daylight, which begins in January in our latitude, affects the migratory impulse of many species, stimulating their reproductive glands and their general metabolism. Still, how do you explain a species that winters in equatorial regions where the length of days remains the same? Evidently the bird's response, if dependent on the influence of light, must have been fixed a long time before the journey to a northern spring, possibly during the previous season before it migrated to the south. Anticipation seems mysteriously built in. I guess birds fly across more years than one.

It may be that terns, travelers like the earth itself, are of the same consistency. They have their inner clocks, their "programmed reactions" to the globe as it shifts its face with respect to the sun. Thinking of migratory terns beating and skipping over the waves, obeying their annual needs, I suppose I must acknowledge mechanism—our own has nearly, if not finally, surpassed human limitations—but that they use the world so well and in their own way, without instruments, taking great distances for granted, thoughtlessly pursuing precise achievements, gave them a long head start over our machines.

Though the marine environment fluctuates, sometimes wildly, with respect to its food supply, from one coastal range to another, the terns arrive when there are sand eels, shrimp, minnows, or other fish fry for them to eat. They rise and go from coasts far to the south as if in response to the rising here, everywhere around us, and in the waters of the sea.

Beginning in March, along with an upwelling of waters rich in nitrates and phosphates, the light increases in intensity and penetrates coastal seas so as to produce a tremendous surge in the reproduction of plants. Microscopic diatoms multiply at such a fantastic rate as to change the color of the sea. The tiny animals of the plankton, the pulsing, whirring drifters, also increase as the sunlight grows stronger and the waters warmer, and graze on the drifting plants. Fish in turn, not passively drifted, but with the power to swim where they want to, move into these areas rich with a new food supply. Arrival is in order, even as wet snow falls in the afternoon and there are freezing temperatures at night.

To see a fish nosing its way upcurrent through the cold waters of an estuary, swaying, a silver water-arrow, a bending of eel grass, a wave, is to see a leader of migration. Each year I ask it seriously what direction I should take.

Sleet after sunlight, then snow or cold rain, followed by southerly winds scattering away the clouds. With formidable dignity, Canada Geese stalk out on the marsh edges, and I hear the sounding gush of waves beyond them where mergansers, soon to leave, are rushing across the surface and diving in. Thunder and lightning follow, down the bowling alleys of the sky, and a roaring April surf. Gray fog covers the shore, with half a sun burning in; gases bubble up through marsh peat and slick mud where mud snails cluster and crawl and the minnows wriggle at low tide, the spring air weaving its acceptances before my eyes.

Perhaps longer daylight affects me physiologically too— I should hope so—while the sunlight softens the ground for fissures by worms and nematodes, and runs through the cellular passages of the frogs. There are shadows before my sight of dancing by light spring flies, and the spider jumps. Each tribe in its time, each inhabitant of every inch of wet or dry ground, counts what is countless by its appearance, and eggs are stirring in that centrifugal response which is the power of spring.

Here under my feet, between the grasses, the oaks, and pines, embryos move, living things display, or, like geese, fly up and V off on major journeys. Under the extravagance we have made of earth—an earth of playtime, fight-time, romanticized and brutalized, a man-made ground where interference is swept aside—under the clatter and roar, mysteriously, since the coordination and regeneration of all earth elements is mysterious, the seeds in soil and water begin to close up and repair all broken and empty spaces. The seeds are in us too, we consumers on top of the pyramid of life who convert its processes to our own use. We are recipients still, part of the global body. We are of streams, rivers, estuaries that preceded our civilized arrival on the scene. We are unwittingly sensitive to our surroundings. We react; we are angered; we hope; we fall by the wayside before some subterranean reality that also moves animals in a tide pool or herds on the run. It is not April's fault if we often show a violent reluctance to equate our reactions with its influence.

Over an island that may be miles out to sea, on overcast days especially, the terns are often heard before they are seen. They fly high overhead as if flirting with the place they flew thousands of miles to reach. Fishermen are likely to meet them days before they finally settle down for good on their nesting islands. I had heard of two pairs being sighted offshore along the coast of New Jersey around April 10, and several off Cape Cod the third week in April.

On April 27, the year before, as I watched the horizon through my fieldglasses, I had seen a number of terns flying in a deliberate way against the wind, miles out over the water. On May 4, according to my notes, light green waters were sketched all over with whitecaps, and there were big, gray, fulsome clouds overhead. Not far off the island in the marsh were several hundred terns, holding up against the strong northwest wind, seeming to float there, then dipping back to the surface and sailing up again. I cried out to them in welcome.

The next day the winds were beginning to calm down, though they were still beating fairly hard along the shore. A few terns were flying down the inlet or tidal creek that ran back through the marsh, and a group of forty was lined up on a sandbar at its mouth, perfectly spaced, a forward-looking, wind-facing phalanx. I noticed one or two craning their heads and necks toward the sky, a hint of more intense mating behavior to come, and there was a single bird standing behind the rest of the flock holding a sand eel in its bill as if it were not sure whom to offer it to.

A few more were fishing in the creek, others were beating their way along the shore, and as I walked out toward the island I could see a big flock on the sand flats several hundred yards beyond. They rose up crying, then settled down again. There were still no birds to be seen over or on the nesting site itself.

When I went back a few days later, I found the terns flying inshore. There was a shore wind blowing, with a trace of England or Africa in it, even of Brazil and Guyana, moving a heavy fog across a dark, brindled marsh that showed only traces of spring green. Terns were racing in and out, appearing and reappearing through the fog with their easy, bouncy flight. They swung back and forth on the down wind. With their graceful tails fanning out and drawing in, they hovered, then twisted and dove into the waters of the creek. "Keearr!" they cried, and then "Kip-kip!" as they slanted off across the ditched, potholed flat marsh and its coarse grass. They beat fast, turning corners, lightly swinging. There was an uplifting to their bodies, to a flight that tested all the buffeting air across the spongy marsh; it took me with them, and the whole sea range seemed to ring with a new mode of attachment.

So I found that the arrival of the terns was gradual, cumulative. Although they roosted at low tide on nearby beaches and peat ledges, or dove for fish, all this in the general neighborhood of the nesting site, they failed to occupy it for some days. After they had arrived offshore, a flock might occasionally fly over the site, then small numbers would land on it temporarily; but it took a while before any of them spent much time there during daylight hours, and it was longer still before they stayed there at night. In other regions along the coastline, large flocks, possibly late, excited, and making up for lost time, might land on an offshore island all at once, coming in from high up, then dropping down and dashing back and forth like a snow squall before alighting.

From the time a few birds, then many more, flocked offshore and began flying over the nesting site, sometimes in a whole flock that moved over it silently and then away again over the water, I had the feeling of rhythmic, accumulating response. At first they showed no prevailing tendency to occupy the territory to which they were drawn and which they had flown so far to reach. In fact, they showed a nervous avoidance of the land. They seemed to roost as far down on the beach as they could, well away from the grasses and sandy hollows where they would lay their eggs. As the tides ebbed, they moved even farther down to the peat and saltwater grasses at sea level. May 10 was the first day I saw the colony, now much increased in numbers, flying back and forth over the site and landing on it, as if it meant to stay.

The motion of the terns seemed wonderfully precise and at the same time had a nerve-sprung, touch-and-go feeling to it. Their elastic bonding with the land came out in this early behavior toward it; flying in, flying away. Then, as their numbers increased and they reinforced the bond with one another in action and feeling, they drew closer. I had seen something like it in schooling fish. It was a classic kind of practice, an organic throw that aimed for a center in the environment it was attracted to, circling, spinning, trying out, drawn in until it succeeded. I thought of "homing" now not just in terms of a pigeon returning to a loft but as a great, dynamic term whose participants defined the nature of the globe.

6

Ritual

Many years ago, I sometimes went along with Reginald Marsh, the painter, on one of his excursions to Coney Island, the Bowery, or the Burlesque in New Jersey after the authorities had thrown it out of New York City. He was a man with a puckish sense of humor who had a great love for crowds in motion, faces with real grain in them, Sunday acrobats on the beach, and girls in every kind of pose. Once when he was sketching calmly in the midst of hundreds of bodies at Coney Island, I made the suggestion that he try sketching them from the water for a change, facing in. Whether or not my idea really made much difference, he gave me credit afterward for a new horizon. It occurred to me one day, far away from that scene, that although I thought I had been looking out for a long time I was really facing in the other direction. I had been wall-watching, facing inward, thoroughly puzzled, with the news of the world in my lap. I had been thinking of the natural earth not for what it was, for its own sake, but as a relief, an antidote, as though I needed continually to apologize for myself and mankind. I did not find it easy to get rid of the apologies, but I began to try, when looking out, to let earth and sea speak for themselves.

It was not the antidotes I looked for now, but unity and the way it revealed and signed itself. I drew a circle in the sand, abstractly, next to the beach grass and its compasses.

A few miles down from the tern colony, in hollows and low dunes behind a beach, were other fundamental signs: stray bones, rabbit pellets, mouse-runs under a plank, a half-eaten Herring Gull, its feathers strewn for yards away. The long sound of the surf, the surest sound in any land, lay steady in the air. How fine it would be to live here truly, in the history of sand, the fragments of bone, the lichen, and the ancient winds. The way man moved off seemed half compulsive, half deceitful to me. Here still, the earth was pared down to essentials. Existence was celebrated in a splinter of driftwood, turned by wind and sand into the shape of an arrow. I saw perfection of form, a state of rest on the way to entering another state, another shift in essential order. But it involved a justice we could not readily agree to.

This is not our style. The minimal, basic adherence is not the human game. We never accepted the backups of creation, the sand grain reduced over millions of years to a nearly final size. Down in the human gut and in the mind is the special torture of knowing change and not really being in control of it. We throw away our courtesy toward natural fittingness, except as we ourselves use or manipulate it. Too much patience is an aggravation.

Even so, natural intricacy and desire never relent on behalf of anything. There are no substitutes, and every blade of grass, every insect emerging, every tree transpiring knows this in its way. "Bow to each other," says the earth, and, "Approach. Sing and find."

Gulls circled and romped together in the air, and below them many others flocked together on the flats, musically calling. A man and his girl went bumping and idling down the beach, swaying together and apart like trees in the wind. I walked out over the complex map of the tidelands, across their ripples and water lanes and shallow pools. It was a silvery landscape, and the sky was sending down light showers like so much sea spray.

Water spurted up from a clam hole. As the tide began to move in, wavelets bobbed and ducked around me, gradually covering and wreathing the ribbed sands. Through my fieldglasses I saw a pair of Common Terns strutting around each other, heads and necks stretched up, tails cocked, wings lowered and held out partly to the side.

Then I noticed two Roseate Terns, recognizable because of their black bills, their longer tails, and feathers of a more uniformly light gray than the Commons'. The stance of these birds is extremely elegant. Their tails project behind them like spars on a sailing vessel. Their velvety gray wings spread out like a cloak, the hem nearly touching the ground, and their shining black heads and beaks point cleanly toward the sky, in a pose that is very formal and proud.

This spring, the ritual of the terns had come to me out of fog, mist, and showers in such a way that I felt as if I had seen the unveiling of a classic style born two thousand years ago; only it was a great deal older than that, and so all the more precious.

I learned that these birds might have been pre-mated, which is to say, paired up the previous year during the breeding season. Either they had spent the winter together after that or they had recognized each other on arriving at their nesting grounds in the spring. Even though most of the pairs that have already mated will do so again, relatively few seem to behave that way when they first arrive, that is, by staying together and courting one another exclusively. After arriving at their territories the majority go through many days of ground and aerial display before the pairs are finally sorted out. If you cannot tell the difference between male and female, as I could not until pairs started to copulate, ten days to two weeks after they arrived, it is hard to know whether males are displaying before females or the other way around. In these early days, three, four, or five displaying together is quite common, which makes distinguishing the sexes even harder.

(I do not know of any ready shortcut to identifying males and females. But in a later year, a warden of a colony of Sandwich and Common Terns on the coast of Great Britain told me he could tell the difference by their voices. Since he had been listening to them all his life, I had no reason to doubt him. He also contended that he could tell male from female by the way the black cap ended at the nape of the neck; it comes to more of a point in the male, and is a little more squared off or blunted in the female. So far, at least, this last distinction has not worked for me, since the shape of the black feathers on their necks seems to depend on the way they happen to be holding their heads, up or down.)

J. M. Cullen, in his thesis on the Arctic Tern,* describes an action he calls "tilting" in the mating display of the Arctic Tern; the behavior of the Common Tern, he says, is almost identical. These and other species have fully devel-

---

* "A Study of the Behavior of the Arctic Tern (*Sterna macrura*)." Thesis deposited at Bodleian Library, Oxford (1956).

oped black caps in the breeding season, but their fall molt leaves them with a streaked or grayish patch on their heads and a whitish forehead; so the black cap presumably has its function. In displaying before a potential mate, a bird will twist its head so that the cap is hidden or partly turned away from its partner; to show it directly seems to have an intimidating effect. If a female walks around a male who is in a "bent" position, with his beak pointed to the ground— as opposed to an "erect" display with head and neck pointed upward—the male on his inside circle makes an effort to keep his cap turned away from her, because if she catches sight of it she might move away.

Since males are probably frightened too, made nervous or put off, by the full display of the cap, and since they are more aggressive than females in their defense of territory, that display may have some significance as a threat, but is probably used more in avoidance and appeasement than as a direct challenge. If a male pecks at a female, or rushes toward her, she will tilt her cap to avoid further trouble, and males startled or frightened by something during a mating display, or while making their way through a neighbor's territory, will do the same.

In ground displays there are two main postures, one erect, with upstretched neck, head and beak pointed vertically toward the sky, the other bent, with neck stretched forward and bill pointed toward the ground; terns often switch abruptly from one to the other. Only a practiced observer with plenty of time to spend is likely to be at all sure of what these postures mean at any given moment, since rival males, unmated females, and young, non-breeding birds all engage in them as well as a pair parading in a courtship that will soon lead to an established nest. According to Cullen, the erect display may be engaged in ". . .

by the female when she visits a male, by the pair when they are courting together, by a bird (male or female) approaching another to get a fish, by a male after surrendering a fish (but not usually after feeding young), by male or female when male dismounts after copulation, by a bird who alights after making a supplanting attack on another, by a bird who must pass through a neighbor's territory to reach its own." In almost all these situations the displaying bird shows some avoidance of another but is either drawn toward it or obliged to pass closer to it.

The bent posture is characteristic of unmated males when they are visited by females but the display is occasionally seen during incubation when the pair comes together. Females occasionally show the posture after pairing, when their males alight beside them after an absence, but they do not use it to advertise for mates.

A male in the bent posture may attack an intruder if it does not respond in a satisfactory way to his display, but this is usually a momentary attitude, changing before any real attack is made.

Understanding their courtship ritual was like attempting to learn the basic positions of the ballet—in idea if not in performance—not impossible perhaps, but seldom mastered late in life. Still, for an amateur, fairly new to the science of behavior, it was an event to discover that what I once thought of as mere billing and cooing actually included tension and the resolution of conflict. Perhaps the terns resolved their conflicts more spontaneously than we did, being less conscious, more obedient to nature. But out of some dark grounds, we shared in basic impulse and elementary need.

However you interpreted those formal gestures of theirs, I saw the same tension, the same restraint, in the way the

Ruffed Grouse drummed or the gulls bowed to each other, and in the way plant life began to spring up in a sequence that measured the days. The rites of spring were real enough. No life lacked ceremony.

The terns reconciled contrary feelings not only during courtship but also as they responded to that in-pulling, half-avoided territory of theirs, from the time they flocked silently over it—like barn swallows reconnoitering a barn before taking possession—to the time they flew out over the water again in August. It was a life-to-earth magnetism whose principles they were acting out. I followed and I tried to learn.

As the month of May progressed, the activity over the island became more intense. At least a few terns were always displaying whenever I visited the colony. One of a pair might be on the ground with wings down and tail cocked, while the other circled over it. Three would land simultaneously, and with necks craned in the same direction and wings in the cloaked courtship position they looked like handsomely uniformed soldiers on dress parade. There would be swift chases going on in the air too, involving three or as many as five or six at a time. They were constantly engaged in flying with one another over the territory, rising up from the sandy hollows and hummocks, leading away, breaking off, settling down again; and day by day the general clamor was increasing.

I watched one Roseate gliding so high in the bright air that I could hardly see it, but its impeccable snowy look made it shine, and the catamaran-like tail feathers showed as two white filaments against the blue. The slightly rosy flush on their breasts that gives these lovely terns their name was not obvious at first, but I could see it when the light was right. Their call is a kind of blurted "Chuwee" or

"Chivy" or "Chuwick," and I heard calls of "Chuk-chuk" or "Gaarh-gaarh" as they flew over in a leisurely way.

With so many birds engaging in courtship flights, I found it even harder to decide what they were doing at any given moment, although certain patterns of flight are to some extent versions of the ground displays. What is basic to these performances is that the males, who choose the location for nesting, must attract females to it by various maneuvers. The process of persuasion takes a good deal of sorting out, and is beset by distractions and interferences. Males do not find a mate immediately unless they are pre-mated, and they may even put a lot of effort into trying to attract birds that may not be the right ones in the first place, such as a male that seems to be behaving momentarily like a female, or a female that is already mated. Either sex recognition takes a while, or it has to wait on an elaborate game. The combination of attack and escape that seems to be a part of all their efforts to get together is also a factor in holding pairs back from the serious business of raising a family. They are edgy, they engage in strict maneuvers, which are broken off, nevertheless, time and time again; but sooner or later, by gradual steps, a female becomes enough interested in a male to keep coming back to his little space of chosen ground and finally to move in for good.

During the second week in May, the Common Terns, which were more numerous on this site than the Roseates, were not as aggressive as they would be later when most of them were nesting. One or two would dive at me when I came too close, but without a great deal of conviction. Once I saw most of the birds that were flying around the island suddenly rise up together, followed by those roosting along the shore, and their crying as a whole sounded more resonant, more even and uniform to me. The unity of the flock is not obvious while so much energy is being spent on pairing up of individuals, but it is always latent, and alarm brings it out again.

Watching terns, I began to see being and place together, more and more, not simply an occupation of one by the other. In their wild and formal exercise, trying over and over, they had an interchange with the sandy land they had come to. Flying fast with one another, pitching up, harshly crying, posturing spontaneously, they had rhythmic alliances with the sharp-bladed beach grasses shaking and whipping in the wind, and with the waters trickling back and forth over the tidal flats, shivering, parting, coming together again under silken clouds.

The sorting out kept increasing in intensity. Displaying pairs pattered around each other in the sand, and I could find a number of chainlike tracks where they had been. After males and females greet each other, a male may walk over to a pre-existing hollow he has chosen, then lower his breast and scratch out backward in the sand. If the female is interested enough, she may go over and stand beside him, or even replace her suitor so as to do a little scraping herself; but this scrape-making early in the season does not necessarily result in final nesting. These scrapes are often only a stage in courtship ritual and some ornithologists have given them the term "false."

I saw much aerial maneuvering as well as ground displays. As I understand them, there are two main types. In one, a male with beak pointed downward, as in the bent display on the ground, tries to lead a female who adopts the erect posture, or a less extreme equivalent of it, with head and neck extended and tilted upward. They fly past each other, each one alternately falling behind and then overtaking the other, so that it looks as if they are swinging together. The second form of display comes when a male and a female make a circling flight high in the air, and then go into a fast downward glide. There are all kinds of variations on these flights, open-ended in their fine, air-running way; I found them very exciting to watch, and to that degree at least, I joined them.

The first type of display is often performed while the male carries a fish in his bill, which apparently adds to his powers of attraction. On the ground, a male dangling a silver fish will be approached by a female who begs for it, making urgent little cries, and sometimes she tries to snatch it away from him, while he makes motions to hold it back. Or he could give her the fish, whereupon she might swallow it promptly and fly away without any signs of gratitude. Or she might hold it in her own beak, while both posture, and then they will suddenly take off in a courtship flight.

A male with a fish might also be joined by some birds that had no legitimate right to beg, such as an unmated bird wanting the fish for its own display, or, later in the season, by birds who could use it to feed young. Any bird with a fish might expect interference. A fish carrier was importuned, stolen from, tricked, and chased at any time in the season, as I found out later. I learned early, by the way, that life in a tern colony was not only full of rhythmic exchanges that were certainly a pleasure to watch, but that common greed, the taking of unfair advantage, and an unavoidable tendency to be petulant, were fundamental too. Not that this did not add a certain accepted and familiar reality to the whole ongoing prospect.

A male without a fish might engage in courtship display
with any female he chanced to meet; as the two of them
went into an aerial flight together, they might be joined by
another cock who would then attempt to take the lead, so
as to attempt an alliance with the same female. Whatever
the combination, display itself attracts and stimulates others
to join in and do likewise.

At times throughout the terns' almost furious maneuvering, I wondered whether any of them would ever be paired
off and get down to the business of serious nesting. Still,
behind all the flying up and breaking away, the constant
interruptions to courtship, there was a passion and a discipline common to all species that drive toward the ends of
survival. Far from being aimless and self-defeating, though
at times they looked that way, these displays were con-
structions of grace and resolution.

As the days went by it seemed to me that I saw more
literal "fish flights" when males actually led with fish in
their bills instead of without them. The fact that many did
not use the fish, in spite of its advantages in attracting
females, might mean that to hold one does inspire too much
interference. I watched a male carrying a fish as he was
being chased furiously by three others. He flew rapidly
back and forth between the sand dunes and the water,
dodging his pursuers all the while, for as much as ten or
fifteen minutes, then he landed in a chosen spot, still carrying a fish but with no partner that I could see.

Another one, followed only lazily by two others, let his
potential mate take a fish where she stood on an offshore
bar exposed at low tide. They stood momentarily together,
posturing; then he flew off, to come back and peck at her a
little, as if to try and chase her from the perch in the direction of the nesting place he had in mind.

I watched one female as she waited on the ground, crying importunately, while a male screeched and postured behind her. Then they were joined by what I took to be her real mate, at any rate, one to whom she seemed more strongly attached, who circled and strutted around her; then they both paused, head up, and flew off together, leaving the other suitor behind.

A male parading with a fish before his prospective mate does a sort of goosestep, breast forward, in a very conscious way. It is an athlete or a soldier strutting his stuff, displaying his medals or his victorious presence before the girls.

(I suspect much of the time spent in finding the appropriate mate might just have an element of critical judgment in it as far as the female is concerned. She needs a mate who is going to bring in plenty of fish and choose a good nesting hollow in the first place. There may not be much conscious choice involved, but it is quite possible that the female has some discriminatory feelings in the matter.

(Earlier in the month I had watched one Common Tern, recognized as a female by her begging cries, as she waited on a shoal of peat beyond the beach, while what I took to be her suitor swept back and forth over the water for a long time hunting fish. He was unsuccessful, and after half an hour or more of no offerings, she flew off and left him. I think much may depend on satisfying her that he is doing enough to catch fish and choose the kind of nesting site she feels is right.)

Often a "fish flight" starts with three or more birds engaged in much sweeping and evasive action, and by a process of elimination it is eventually resolved into two. The remaining pair then goes into the regular mode, with the birds interchanging positions. The bird in front may

swing downward and to the left, while the other flies over
and past it, and then the procedure is reversed as the bird
now in the lead moves back and downward, with bowed
wings beating just a little. There is a lovely, tilting balance
to their flight. The male sounds a clear *"Keera,"* while the
female may cry "Kip-kip" or "Tik-tik"; and then his call
may change to a rasping "Koh-koh-keearrh."

So the sorting out in the colony went on and on, and I
heard many other cries as the birds went through their
nearly incessant flying up and landing again, many stri-
dently challenging, bonding, connective cries. Isn't this
urgent relating and re-relating, for days on end, analogous
to what we are continually required to do, though sometimes veering wildly, forcibly, even madly, in the wrong
direction?

The more I saw of courtship flights, the more they
compared with human games. The natural ease of great
ballplayers was in them, of champion skaters or ballet
dancers. At the same time I doubt whether much in the
natural world can equal the high flights and their glides. A
high flight usually takes place between a male and a female
only, and involves circling upward until they reach a high
altitude, with one leading the other. At some point one of
the birds folds its wings slightly and starts to glide in an
easy way toward the ground, while the other follows; the
two of them bank back and forth from one side to the
other, swaying and side-slipping together as if their whole
life had been a training for such an act.

The Roseate Terns, a cut in elegance above the Commons, have a beautifully reaching look to their bodies as
they glide together. When a pair fly slowly together over
the ternery, their wings, stroking with a thoughtless assurance that seems to measure clouds and waves, appear to

lean and hang on the air, their forward edges marking lines
of accommodation to it. Pairs of terns of both species will
circle high over the territory, but the Roseates often fly
directly out over the sea in a great circling fetch, and are
then lost to sight. Once I saw a pair of Roseates, way
overhead, in a strong wind, that looked as if they were
flying backward as they ascended, and at the same time
they were perfectly in control. Their skill was dazzling.
With Common Terns, and Roseates, a very fast chasing
and circling upward often ended in a wide zig-zagging
glide.

Roseate Terns arrive on the nesting grounds somewhat
later than the others, and also start nesting later. So in the
middle of June, after most of the Common Terns are
incubating eggs, or brooding their chicks, groups of Roseates are still engaged in fast courtship flights. There is
nothing more beautiful to me than a group of these terns
racing ahead, slip-streaming through the sky, incomparably
lithe and limber, dynamically turning as they go. At times
they skate through the sky as if shot from a sling, and at
others they sail and float as buoyantly as a kite on a high
wind; or they knife quickly through the air like mackerel
in undulant waters. They remind me then of Blake's
"arrows of desire."

The Roseate Terns, which even on the ground have a
more nervously erect and speedy look to them, do indeed
go into higher and faster flights, but both species make
spectacular glides. At times, after a passage of synchronized
swinging, they appear to start tumbling or revolving high
in the air, which is apparently due to a form of gliding in
which they turn as they fall, tilting one wing above the
other on a vertical instead of a horizontal plane. Whereas
Common Terns may start a downward glide from about

five or six hundred feet and Roseates from still higher, Sandwich Terns will circle up to several thousand feet. I am told that from that great height a pair of them will drop at a speed of sixty or seventy miles an hour, both birds sliding with wings out, the pressure on their outer primaries making a papery, drumming sound. They plunge downward toward the ternery at an angle of about sixty degrees until they are within three or four hundred feet of the ground, then sheer upward again to circle back and land, in an easy and finished way, together. The whole arc of this masterful performance might take in as much as two miles. What a surpassing way to express the feeling of two beings who are free to recognize each other's sex!

Every time I walked once again across the marsh to the island, I could see long, high, well-coordinated flights up in the smoky, feathered sky, and pairs going into that switching, almost pendulum-like glide together, to land and posture in their stylized way. Or I would see two birds follow the fish carrier in cross-swinging flight until one left off while the remaining pair continued on in measured juxtaposition.

A friend of mine once said to me, as I was rhapsodizing about birds: "How does that relate to me? Tell us about *ourselves*." Hadn't I yet shown him parallels enough? I realize that very few of us, even when about to be married, have the ability to launch into paired aerial maneuvers a thousand feet up. Having lived so long, to tell you the truth, I am none too clear about what all the practice we can and do indulge in goes for: to keep the structure of society intact, meanwhile increasing our means of destroying its room and resources at the same time? Still, nature rules us. What you come to realize, after living in one place long enough, is the extent to which men and women depend on each other's hostility—not too fearsome a term when it is resolved into such vital elements as keeping your position, your self-respect, your opinions, and your likes and dislikes with relation to everyone else. It can't be done alone. Every town is in some respects a miserable one, because everyone in it nurses feelings—and birds need those feelings too.

Terns are nervous and excitable creatures, and in their existence love, as we aspiringly define it, is apparently only an incident in their lives, one which, if relevant, is to a high degree made up of aggravation. Those almost unending starts and chases of theirs during the breeding season are all flights toward a resolution. An order is observed in their drive to reproduce, as it is by salmon, by alewives, and by deer in the rutting season. But in a community of terns— males and females trying to relate, to set up housekeeping and produce offspring, all in a very short season—the process often looks quite frenzied. Yet perhaps they are only as persistent and as compulsive in their way as human beings acting on imperative inner demands throughout their own lives. Which is more unconscious than the other?

I grew almost dizzy at times with trying to decode their various maneuvers. Wild chases, seemingly angry flights with much noise would be resolved into a breaking off between two rival males, or as temporary pairs were formed, either in the air or on the ground. I could never be quite sure what was happening. Every action had some element of attack, of hesitation and withdrawal. Even these culminative high flights were not entirely without ambivalence. Such a flight might start between two males, and certain aspects of it, such as the way one bird swooped at another as the two began to ascend, made it look like a chase. At times the traces of hostility to be found in any courtship performance gave way to something like real conflict. I saw one pair in a flight that seemed to start off easily enough, but all at once they dipped quickly toward the ground, with angry, gargling cries, in a flurry of beating wings. Or, two birds, wings stroking rapidly, would rise from the ground, partly turning around each other and moving backward at the same time. The one would rise above the other, and they would keep alternating in this way, each trying to be the one on top. It was an action that had some of the characteristics of a fight between two males on the ground, but often turned into a paired flight that looked like courtship. These "flutter-ups" are mainly associated with nesting territory, and play some part in the recognition by individual birds of their separate claims—which leads to the idea that they are probably engaged in by males.

I saw a vigorous fight going on between two male Roseates on the ground. They pecked violently at each other, wings beating and flurrying, but broke off after a few seconds. In behavioral terms, it might be said that the fight had served to define a mutual tolerance, a recognition that could be translated into a few inches of territory.

The bond of feeling and of place was in all their actions. When I saw two birds flying straight upward, a miniature funnel of wings that spiraled in the air, I felt the force in them, made up of the pull and weight of the ground below and their own angry energy. Up they went, out of sight, drifting away, bound to return.

I got the impression that flutter-ups took place quite often where birds were newly establishing nests in areas not preempted. On the other hand, I saw one bird flying and fluttering low over another that was sitting on a nest, as though trying to take it over. The second was bothered enough to fly up, and an angry, fluttering rise began, which was interrupted as the first bird flew off with a third, perhaps its mate, and the nest sitter went back to business. It must be, I thought, that these terns need each other to resolve a good many uncertainties!

The colony became more wildly clamorous as the days passed, though noise and activity were muted during bad weather. Territorial maneuvering and courtship go on in the rain, but at a slower tempo. One lady observer told me that Roseate Terns are very shy about making love in the rain. Stormy weather unquestionably holds down the fish flights and the high ascents and glides. Heavy fog restricts them too.

The third week in May started with heavy rains, followed by fog and drizzle, and I did not get back to the colony until the eighteenth, which was a fine, clear day. Most of the favored sites were in the center of the territory and were now occupied, but some birds, nesting later, had settled down to incubate eggs in the sand on the outer perimeters. These terns now started swooping in my direction, with threatening cries. Aggressiveness toward intruders, half-hearted at first, grows more intense as nesting advances. Male Common Terns will fly at you, almost close enough to get a good crack at your skull, with a low "ahn-ahn-ahn" of annoyance that turns into a rasping, staccato "kek-kek-kek-kek-kek." Occasionally a tern may hit you and even draw blood. Terns also let their droppings fly at you, and since some of them are very successful at finding the mark, it is a good idea to wear a hat. Roseate Terns, on the other hand, are less aggressive birds; they will make low flying approaches, sounding a slightly less harsh "Kaagarrh-kaarh," but they veer off sooner than the others, without coming in close to attack.

"Keep your distance!" was the cry; but for all their alertness and, if translated into human terms, their pluck and valiance, I thought of how terribly hard it is for non-human life to talk that way to men and be respected.

I walked out over the marsh on another day, intending to watch the birds from a distance that would not disturb them too much. A faint smell of fish came to me on a warm wind along the shallow waters of the shore. On the way, I saw a tiny, wiggling elver at the edge of the tidal creek, materializing as if nothing like it had ever swum into my sight before. A triumphant novelty had arrived, coming from a nature so fecund and at the same time so coolly enigmatic as to elude all conscious description. I had come from watching alewives again as they ran and crowded in to spawn, thinking that if they were human they might pant and die from the effort to understand what they were doing.

Creative anonymity moved the spring. The marsh with its dun-colored grasses and winding inlets, its pitted banks, had an indolence of its own that it shared with space. I heard the deep, alarmed quacking of a Black Duck; then a Song Sparrow with a spitting, spurting kind of melody. A few Brant, with rolling gait, were slowly working over the marsh grasses. These small geese have beautifully shaped heads, like the statuette of an Egyptian queen or a Greek goddess. And Piping Plovers, whose colors faded into sand, scuttled and stopped, scuttled and stopped, on the beach in front of the nesting island.

The same adjusting and agitation was going on through all the hummocks and hollows, and the air was full of cries. Terns started toward each other and then broke off. They flew with quick wing-beats or slowly and deliberately. Sometimes their wings, during courtship on the ground, were lifted in a V instead of hanging like a cloak at their sides. The tempo of their cries shortened or lengthened, and the sounds I heard from individual birds were harsh, excited, and rasping, or sometimes almost smooth and watery. Everywhere I saw action, intent, and the expectation of reciprocal action. This was not a simple but an intricate society, tense with preparation. I saw a perpetual trying in them, which men might term bird-minded and small, a kind of spontaneous tripping of nerve ends, but even if I were to accept that judgment I was always conscious that they were acting to the measure of some greater, infinitely complex ceremonial—and the breath of the tides around them declared it too.

By this time, toward the end of May, the majority of pairs had reached the point of nesting and incubating eggs. (Courtship behavior, incidentally, can be seen all through the summer, because there are usually a certain number of young, unmated birds and even occasional strays from other colonies, such as pairs that might have deserted their nests in spring or early summer and are now trying again. Shifting between nesting areas is rare with individuals, as distinct from the wholesale desertion of a colony, but it has been known to occur, at times from fairly distant points.)

I watched several sequences that must, after many days of trial, have been nearly final. A female, slightly hunched down, her beak wide open, was begging in front of a male who held a fish. When she suddenly grabbed at it, he flew off, as if to say: "You do it right, or we don't get together at all." To put it in the abstract, her slight aggressiveness might have been disturbing to the exactness they needed to bond them surely, a bond that was reinforced by two needs: the one in her to lay eggs and in him to start to nest. But that is to underemphasize the extraordinary nervousness that seems to run through their courtship. The inner testing that marks these attempts to pair up, even in their final stages, means that the male may be just as frightened as the female, or enough afraid of her so as not to surrender his fish.

As I watched them, far away as they were from my own reality, I sensed the kind of ambivalence or uncertainty that was vaguely analogous to my own at times in the past. Seasons of hesitation, nerves sprung in the wind, characterized us both. I even thought that on a deeper level all their concentrated effort, with its often wayward rhythms, might be directed toward a certainty in experience whose search also brought energy into man's affairs and fear to his heart.

Roseate Terns, as compared with the Commons, which like more open ground, choose fairly thick vegetation to nest in, often making small tunnel-like openings at the edge of a heavy growth of grass. In some areas they also nest under boulders or in rock burrows where they are narrowly confined and where mating rituals have to be performed in a very stylized and precise manner. The male goes in first, followed by the female, who starts facing him, then pivots around, head and tail up, while he lowers his head, calling "Uh-uh-uh-uh." Then the female goes back out while he engages in some scraping motions. Terns know where their boundaries are, though they may be invisible to us, especially out in the open; but rock walls obviously enforce proximity, and it seems that the ritual has to be precisely carried out or the pair will fight.

Since the Common Terns were out in the open, I could watch them more readily than I could the Roseates, observing them at some distance through my fieldglasses. One morning I saw a male Common Tern fly in with a fish and then let his mate take it. She promptly ate the food and this apparently provided the right stimulus because he then copulated with her. Not far away from them, another male flew down to a begging female and they both postured. Then he circled around her, first in one direction and then in another, four or five times over, while she turned only slightly; after which he mounted her, standing high on her back for a minute or two, and then lowered to copulate. Then he stretched his head and neck a little and they both flew off. During the action another bird stood close by, posturing a little with a sort of half-hearted but hopeful intent, as though he—I assumed it was a male—entertained the notion of mounting her too. For terns, three is not always a crowd. In fact, I heard of a case in which an unmated male joined a pair that was already engaged in incubating eggs and was allowed to help. The married couple just got used to having him around, apparently, and then gave him the key.

Efforts at copulation don't always succeed right away. A male may mount a female and stand on her back for minutes at a time in an absentminded, half-hearted way before he climbs off, with nothing accomplished. Repeated efforts are often made, but with consummation egg laying soon follows.

Watching in another direction, I saw one bird enlarge a scrape just a little, digging out backward while his mate stood aside. Then he stood back while she moved in to the nesting site plucking lightly at some grass. Finally both postured, circling each other, and then stood on the nest together, facing into the wind with an air of proud attachment.

7

A Central Place

An island not more than a few hundred yards long and fifty feet wide supports only a relatively limited number of birds. Part of it was too thickly vegetated to suit the Common Terns, and some areas were made unusable for both species by piles and windrows of thatch thrown in by storm tides. There were about thirty-eight hundred terns there, six hundred of them Roseates.

This colony was protected. There were signs on the beach reading *Keep Off. Nesting Birds.* Protection was needed in a county that was said to be the second fastest growing in the nation. The capacity for natural interchange in the area seemed to be giving way to human occupation. When I traveled, I often had to look for wildlife in a refuge, even though as resources it ought to be part of our existence. Did I have to accept the world as a farm of aphids tended by human ants?

But I thought that even to post a sand spit was to recognize an obligation. We were obligated to an exchange between living things; we were obligated to planetary space where life could thrive. Our own vitality required it, in many senses. The tern colony on its little island had connections that went far beyond this local shore. How could the Arctic Tern nesting on some small island in the wet tundra, far north of here, have any proper refuge but the earth itself, if its needs included a migration of 12,000 miles?

The terns do not sort out through mind and speech the reasons for their choice of a nesting site. The rituals they carry out all through the breeding season are innate, known ahead of time by the whole society, for the whole society, already prepared in the nervous system of the individual. The knowing in them predates the accomplishment of conscious learning; it is a mystery behind mystery, behind things still unaccounted for by science, and it is always drawn to a basic place.

This place, for example, girded by tidewater twice a day, its buff and white sands held down by runners of beach grass whose limber, switching leaves serve as indicators of the force of the wind. It is a semi-desert. During hot days in the summer, the surface of the bare sand reaches extreme temperatures. So the Terns have to brood their newly hatched chicks constantly. Nights during early spring can be very cold, and raw storms out of the north that pick up moisture out of the sea can strike unmercifully. Plants such as the beach pea curl up their leaves on days of intense sunlight so as to conserve moisture, and others are modified in various ways to cut down on evaporation. In this place are holes and tunnels made by meadow voles that scurry out now and then to nibble seeds. Do they disturb the terns? Only mildly, I would guess. Rats, where they occur, are a terrible menace, and occasionally snakes eat eggs or young. Even ants may get inside of a tern's egg and destroy embryo or unhatched chick.

One day I found several terns with the heads torn off, and I knew that the colony had been raided by a Great Horned Owl. Not many days after, in fact, I heard from a man who had been out in his boat after dark and had seen a big flock of terns fly off with much crying from the island, remaining on the water for some time, and it is possible that an owl could have unnerved them. A hawk lingering in the area of a ternery can result in a nearly constant state of anxiety. When such a hawk comes into their sight again, groups of terns may suddenly take off, deserting their nests, wheeling out over the water and then returning again, sometimes with a loud outcry; or they may do this spontaneously simply because the enemy is still there, though not in view.

Silent flights, as opposed to noisy ones at the approach of an intruder, seem to be always latent in a colony of terns, and often take place with no apparent cause. Once I saw a small group on a beach fly out silently and then back again for no reason, unless it could have been a wave that smacked the sands with unusual sharpness, as waves do at intervals on a changing tide. A man or a dog will sometimes jump like that too, but with terns, which act together, it is not just a matter of being startled. These silent "outflights" of theirs have a certain eerie quality, so that they have been given the term "dreads." "Panics" is another designation, or "alarms," though an alarm flight, if the distinction is allowable, may be accompanied by an outcry.

A sudden noise, an unexpected movement, even the sight of a single bird flying quickly and abruptly out to sea, may send up at least part of the colony. For a second or two, their normal volume of crying decreases, then, suddenly, with as much discipline as a flock of sanderlings or starlings, they wheel out over the water, with only the sound of their whishing wings to be heard.

Panics, and once again, I am not quite sure of the distinction, may occur like this: the sudden blast of a boat horn is heard offshore, whereupon the entire colony rushes up silently, to wheel and swerve over the water, its members dashing and falling like autumn leaves. As an integrated flock they then dive low across the surface, rise up into the wind, and return to their territory, though they may not settle down until after several of these wild forays. One observer at a tern colony in Britain told me that at times high-frequency sounds going through a ternery can cause a panic—even snapping your fingers may do it—and that such a panic sometimes occurs a couple of days before the onset of a storm, indicating, I suppose, a certain nervous sensitivity in terns that might be associated with changes in the weather. He made a distinction between major panics and "pockets" of them made by small groups and occurring throughout the season.

A common element in these flights is that they take place over the water, conspicuously avoiding the land, just as they do when the terns first arrive. Ornithologists assume that since the water provides escape from predators, as the land does not, the birds' reaction is a sign of fear. They fly downward toward the water at first, as though a hawk were chasing them, and they also flock together more closely than usual—as is characteristic of birds in general, and of other species of animals. Schooling fish, for example, bunch together when they are being pursued or when they are suddenly alarmed.

Most silent outflights, on the other hand, are not caused

by predators at all. In fact, both Common and Arctic Terns are so aggressive that they are more likely to mob a predator than fly away from it, though a Great Horned Owl in the dark may be an exception. It is also worth noting that continued outflights later in the season may coincide with prolonged disturbance or an exceptional lack of food, and could signal an early departure from the ternery.

These flights occur under so many different conditions, and often for such apparently contradictory reasons, that it is hard to assign them a function. They belong to the still undeciphered nature of a tern, and this gives them a special fascination.

The incidence of dreads, panics, or alarms—in other words, outflights—seems also to vary a great deal, from colony to colony and from year to year. In some areas these "pockets" may occur throughout the season, and in others they are very few. Perhaps a distinction can be made between an outflight consisting of a number of birds flying off spontaneously for no apparent reason (or none more notable than the appearance of other birds flying in their direction and leading them out, as it were) and one that has some clearly audible or visible cause. Such outflights seem to occur most often either early or late in the breeding season, especially during the early morning or evening. It is hard to classify them.

Modes of response such as this might be assigned a meaning, given enough observation, but since they are part of the "psyche" of the animal—I do not find a better term— each variation is unique and probably has as many functions as there are occasions to produce them. Silence as a condition communicates itself spontaneously among the terns, and perhaps is one means by which their basic unity is maintained during the breeding season. But their strangely silent, abrupt departures always seemed to me to be less a matter of the specific functions they might serve than a kind of showing of psychic energy, patterns unknown.

What *is* that nervous force I saw in terns, or in migrant fish schooling and swerving away with such a quickness in them? How could I name it? Is it mindless, or does it imply something more than that, a mode of communication having some realizable connection with cause and effect?

Fear is involved, I feel fairly sure. Fear takes its part in crowd communication and makes the fishes swerve. It is latent in me, and it is intrinsic to whatever drives men's enormous efforts to protect themselves against nature. In a sense all technology serves this purpose. But fear, either as we or the terns might know it, is not only a matter of running away from things, but of sensing the most profound relationships woven through the air, the ground, and the water where we move.

Another place, another working out of the same signals, further obedience to the same mysteries. One weekend in late May I visited Great Gull Island, a research center maintained by the American Museum of Natural History, about an hour's trip by boat from the Connecticut shore. The island had been used as a fort from the time of the Spanish-American War but had been abandoned following the Second World War. Ten years later the terns, whose habitat on the shores of Long Island Sound had been restricted by developments, factories, public parks, and beaches, began to use the island for nesting. Their numbers increased so that in the early 1970s there were altogether about seven thousand Common and Roseate Terns there.

We approached Great Gull toward sundown over molten copper waters. The buildings of the old fort almost completely covered the little island, with flat concrete walls and roofs hunkered down between grassy shoulders. To stabilize the shoreline, the Army had covered it with huge boulders, or traprock. As the island became distinguishable the terns showed up as white, scattered chips sailing in the air, and as we came closer still, their gargling, harsh cries sounded through the wind and the lapping of waves.

Here was that same fierce exercise I had watched on Cape Cod; the tribe of terns was at its synchronized work of survival. There was the same flying back and forth in mutual excitement, the individual efforts to lead, the continual falling short and trying again. Because the number of birds on this island was so much greater than the one I already knew, the drama here seemed heightened. Also, I would be spending the night in the midst of the colony, instead of having to cut my visit short.

That first night was wide out with its sea air and the stars. With empty windows, abandoned streets and installations, the ruined fort was like an American Pompeii, and I could hear terns whenever I woke up during the night. There were scattered cries from the near end of the island, and now and then an abrupt "Kraak!" or "Keeat" would sound overhead, with the timbre of a comb plucked by the fingers, as a single bird or a pair swept over the roofs and past the walls. It was a resonant, almost imperious cry, across a night massed with starry directions.

There is reason to believe that terns are noisier on clear or moonlit nights. In fact, they may do some offshore fishing when the moon is shining. I was told by a photographer there, incidentally, that if you shine a flashlight or use a photographic flash against a flock roosting on a dark night, it apparently makes them lose their sense of distance, foreshortening it, and they begin excitedly and aggressively flying at one another, showing an emotional instability, though I don't suppose there is much in their evolution that prepared them for flashbulbs.

It may be that after a colony has become stabilized in one territory over a period of years, there will be less of a racket, especially at night, than in one that is still growing and settling in. In other words, if terns occupy a new island, the chicks hatched there will not breed consistently until they are fully mature. Some terns breed when they are two or three years old, but the majority breed at four. An island with relatively less mature and paired-up terns on it, preoccupied with incubating eggs and brooding chicks, will be a great deal less quiet. It is quite possible too that such a colony would engage in fewer outflights.

Those birds as I heard them still leading and pursuing called me out too under the star-pitted sky. I got up out of my sleeping bag, walked out onto the empty street, and was made dizzy by the vast heights beyond me, heights that could direct a bird on its migration. A tern for a star. Surely, I thought, they must know the constellations when migrating on a clear night, whatever else was in them to define and correct their course, and know them better than I did. This ancestral race embodied the reaches of the world. What could it be but strict in its motions, intense in its performance, with such great standards to follow?

I heard "Keearr" now as a major tribal cry, and I put it off against our scattered mechanical thunder and human spreading on the farther shore. If we based our civilization wholly on the premise that we could neutralize or dissolve the high risk all nature requires of its lives, were we really protecting ourselves?

I thought of human crowds, the numbers in us and around us interminably adjusting and crying out, and there might be some analogy there with colonial birds. "What people say," as contrasted with what individuals, trying to make a world of their own, are able to express, is part of a natural tumult. On the other hand, I thought of all of us with our superior brains, in an unsettled world, shifting between applied reason and violently misapplied emotion, as having connections with our natal earth that were decidedly uneasy. Can this ship of civilization, orbiting in its own space, be controlled by conscious effort, or is there another passion in us, moving us, that has no outcome to reveal? The universe hatches great desires, both intricate and cruel.

Great Gull Island was another variation in identity. The Terns made scrapes in gravelly ground, on bare stretches where the fort's concrete was exfoliating, or along stony parts of the beach. The Roseate Terns often nested deep between the crevices of the traprock. When the research staff and their weekend helpers made daily nest checks there, they had to contort their backs and stretch their necks to capacity. Instead of having its back to a salt marsh, the island was far out on the water, swept around with tidal rips and currents, within the sound of fog horns, whipping winds, planes overhead, and water breaking against its rocky shores. With sea music glinting and booming out of open light, I watched a group of terns as they stood facing

Roseate Terns cruise over their nesting sites in heavy island vegetation. Common Terns choose barer spots, often sandy places between clumps of Beach Grass.

After the eggs are laid they are incubated almost continuously, by females and males in turn.

After sitting, the bird often indulges in preening—considered by many ornithologists as a conflict gesture between the urge to brood the eggs and a desire to desert the nest.

Eggs and chicks may be washed away, killed by exposure if the adults fail to brood them, or eaten by predators—signs of the extreme risk in which all life engages.

Terns fly short distances at three or four weeks, fish for themselves at about nine weeks. To the observer, their first spontaneous flights over the water come unexpected—arrived at gradually.

Frequently one catches sight of high-flying adults, overlapping, swinging back and forth, passing over and under each other in an easy, loping interchange.

The tern's life remains a richness of interaction and expression. Compared to their employment of natural endowments, I feel unused, lazy and indifferent. *(Photographs by Gordon S. Smith)*

into a twenty- to thirty-mile-an-hour wind, streamlined, stiff as weathervanes, hunched down, their heads and necks pulled in. Occasionally the wind would throw them off balance; their tail ends teetered up and they had to readjust themselves, with a fussy tucking and retucking of their wings. The pure black on the crown of their heads curved down to the nape of their necks, cloths of distinction. Occasionally, one of them would fly up and hang on the force of the air for a while.

On this home ground they seemed even more intimately connected with the roll of the seas, lifting and wind-conducted across the wrinkled waters, roving away. Weather of all kinds was their medium. I had seen them now, here and on the Cape, through curtains of dawn, in cold rain, lightning and hail, or against a rippling, fiery sea at sundown. All their swooping and chasing, swerving and gliding, was part of a ceremony rhythmically allied with the stretching, shallow seas along the coast and the open oceans where they followed their transverse migratory routes.

I thought of sea birds profoundly oriented to the dark, gray-green distances over which they soared, having the magic feeling in them of global reach. The way the planet heeled was in their flight, the way it raced. There must have been an unquestioning reliance in them on all that is.

The world to a tern would not be one with many seas that can be offset by your scrutiny and put on a map, but an inner equivalent known long before "discovery." As well as the stars, they followed girdling runs of islands, inlets, or farther inland lakes and marshes; they followed warm or cold air and the visible food in the waters, all of which their kind knew well. It was the intruder like me, who could see the world as a whole and at the same time have it slip away from him, who had partly lost this common but deep ability to find his way.

We speed ahead, with a marvelous lack of inner confidence. It is as if, on this global home, an inherited possessiveness in us had more power; was more formidable than any of our trajectories into empty space. Ignorant of what moves us, we lay claim to the whole planet. I saw how the terns, more precise about their chosen ground, ready in their perfect wings to meet variety, coming on again to fish and breed so as to suit an ever-changing earth, were, in a sense, on this island ahead of us, staking out legitimate claims. We needed their wisdom. To dispossess them in too many places would be to destroy a genius in essentials.

A tern needs a place to breed in that offers a reliable source of food nearby and is relatively free from predators. *We* say we require . . . practically everything. Except for the poor, the food is not just fish and potatoes. Still a basic place, whether it is New York City, New Delhi, or one of those wild and open seaside ranges I have grown to love, imposes its own requirements on both human and non-human life. There must be order. There must be balanced community. There must be mutual use of resources among friends as well as enemies, prey or predator, and there must be rituals.

For me, entering into a new landscape is not too different from entering a human company I have never met before. It takes time to learn what is there, to sense the inner shifts and changes around me, to feel out sympathies and rejections that have their equivalents in me. I begin to sound the depths.

With the feeling not so much of leaving the tern island in

the marsh as of adding to it, I made a two-week trip to Europe in June. I visited Laesø, an island in northern Jutland, with Sigurd Bruhn, an ornithologist friend from Copenhagen. He was a fine guide, not only because he knew the area, but because he loved it, especially in springtime when the birds were nesting. We went by ferry to where the island lay in shallow seas. The tides there were negligible compared with those of Canada and New England; we walked offshore for hours through low water, hardly noticing its rise and fall. On one side of the island were grassy islets like stepping stones, one beyond the other, and in between them rocks stood out like minor megaliths.

These islets were full of breeding birds. Of the terns there were the Sandwich, a few Gull-billed, and a scattering of the Arctic and the Common. The region also had Oystercatchers, European Avocets, shelducks and eiders, Common and Black-headed Gulls, each kind on its chosen nesting and feeding grounds—grassy, sandy, or stony, on bank or flat—with some, like the Gull-billed Tern, showing a preference for lower, wetter places. The Sandwich Terns nested here in close flocks, grouped in two main areas, and when disturbed they rose in a concentrated mass of beating white and silver wings, making a canopy overhead. Common Terns were few in number, with scattered nests on smaller islets. The Arctics were also scattered in small groups, over grassy meadows closer to shore. I caught sight of one of their half-grown, blue-gray chicks as it moved away to hide in the grass. In other parts of Europe where the populations of the two species are denser, they are sometimes more closely associated.

The Gull-bills feed more on insects than on fish, though they eat freshwater animals such as frogs, and are often found near inland ponds and marshes. In Europe they occur more commonly in latitudes to the south of Denmark. This colony was at the northernmost limit of their range, and was probably a remnant one, barely hanging on. The terns had been disturbed recently by local picnickers, whose children had taken the eggs and thrown them around, or enjoyed themselves shifting them from one nest to another. This had caused one of the two groups of Sandwich Terns to desert their nests and try again on another little island not far from the first.

I had begun to learn some of the differences among species of terns, variations on the ancestral theme: size and color, length of tail, shape of bill and wings, and specialized physical characteristics became clearer to me; but what really struck me as we wandered on, surrounded by terns flying, flocking, and sitting on their nests, not to mention other species of birds, was the depth of associated life that I began to feel around me.

Terns with high trilling laughs, such as the Gull-billed, Sandwich terns sounding a little like frogs with their occasional "Rek-rek," terns rising all at once, or singly, or which brooded unseen on their nests in the grass, took part in an intricate web of response. I sensed a timing, unknown to me, in all the birds that moved or raised their wings as I passed. I guessed at unknown ranges of signaling between them. I felt a continual testing out by them of their surroundings. This low-lying seaside land was their intimate, and who knows how they responded to all its changes?

On still another side of the island, where we walked the following day, there was a wide beach. Ridges of sand had been pushed in to the head of the beach by storm tides, and behind that lay a gray swale of pebbly and sandy ground and then a stretch of small rippling dunes held down by beach grass. We came there to look for Least Terns. Watching from the dunes, we finally saw two pairs settling down in a pebbly area and we walked out to look for the eggs, while the birds dipped back and forth over our heads, with cries of alarm. Having located one nest with eggs in it, I walked away and barely avoided stepping on another one, in which there was a newly hatched chick, a mere flicker of yellow on the ground, that might have been a chip of wood or a bunch of dried grass. It was not much over two inches long, with fine dark tracings on its tiny back, of a beige color, tinted with honey from the sunlight. The chick seemed completely helpless and unprotected on that bare ground, and I might have feared for it; but its parents were ardent in its protection, and I knew that an exposure that looked perilous to a man meant all that was reliable to a tern.

As we walked back in the late afternoon across short-grass meadows, called "Strand Eng" by the Danes, Oyster-catchers were crying out noisily and monotonously, "Kteep! Kteep! Kteep!" An avocet with broad wings and showy black and white plumage did a broken-wing act to lead us away from its nest—it almost seemed to know what a striking effect it had. Who could help being distracted by such a display! A dark kestrel suddenly swooped down toward a nestling in the grass, and a pair of Arctic Terns shot up, crying harshly, and drove it away. A pair of Turnstones stood stolidly out in the open, but with a look of extreme alertness. I had the feeling of watchful eyes and senses everywhere. The place was full of guardians, senti-nels, and protectors. So while the birds gave their paper-tearing, shrill, or whistling cries, we left the Strand Eng, grass woven, sea fibered, behind, waiting for the wild and ancient, copper-tinged twilight to come in.

Many of the birds that nest in these meadows are closely associated. Turnstones, for example, nest where there are terns, and nowhere else. Out on the islets, another kind of region, one can find a Common Gull's nest right in the middle of a closely packed group of Sandwich Tern nests. In the same vicinity European Eiders lay their eggs quite close to where Herring Gulls and Lesser Black-backed Gulls nest. Sometimes the presence of a larger species serves to protect a smaller one, but if an eider leaves its eggs or chicks uncovered they are only too likely to be seized and eaten by its neighbors the gulls. In the face of such a disaster, these sea ducks will doggedly lay their eggs all over again in the same place.

My two-week trip included several days in Britain, and there I saw eiders and Arctic Terns nesting together on one of the Farne Islands. A number of the terns were nesting in bare spots surrounded by clumps of grass on the slopes that led up from the beach. Others were nesting on the beach itself, among rocks and seaweed. I also saw a good many "off-duty" terns resting and preening along the shore.

A few eider ducks nested on higher ground, and when they came back from a feeding expedition on the water they had to pass among the terns as they waddled up the beach. I watched one female hesitating for a long time at the water's edge, moving forward a little, stopping, then trying it again, while the terns cried out like hecklers from the sidelines. As she waddled slowly and bravely up the beach, the closer she got to the bank the more excited they became. They began screaming and diving at her, continually hitting her with their droppings. One might admire their aim, incidentally, but terns are not archers as far as defecation is concerned. They let fly when they are anxious and excited. Their anxiety rises when they dive at an intruder, and man or eider suffers the results.

So she moved on, slowly but steadily, ducking her head and body all the time under the unremitting bombardment. By the time she reached the top of the bank her reddish-brown body was splattered white with lime.

Along the Scottish coast farther north, I looked down on the sea beating at the base of craggy cliffs, whose ledges and crevices were filled with nesting kittiwakes, auks, and guillemots. Thousands of these birds poured across the surface of the sea and rested on it. The sound of the ocean waters swashing in and out of caves in the rock, pouring around rocky headlands, welling in and backing off, added to the roaring clamor of the birds, each one whining, barking, or crying, had a mesmerizing power. There was danger there too, of an irreducible kind.

The ground where living things associate is as much defined by risk as protectiveness. The kestrel goes after a tern chick; the Gull-billed Tern steals the eggs of other birds; gulls chase terns to make them drop the food they are bringing to their young; and terns of the same colony do that to one another. Danger is everywhere, but it is woven into the vitality of the ground.

Friends and enemies are found in any community, and since there is a strong element of intimidation in all court-ship, there is love and war among couples too. The relent-less and persistent need to reproduce their kind holds terns, gulls, and ducks to the same place, the same fabric of fear and patience. This is primal attachment. A salt marsh, a short-grass meadow, a sea cliff, or sea island, patiently receiving harsh and icy storms, or threaded through with spring desire, does not speak for "wildlife" in our sense of the term but for life, wild wherever it is.

8

Communication

I was surprised to find that basic language and even occasional intonations in speech were very much alike in Scandinavia and the British Isles. The Scotch sometimes sounded like the Danes, and vice versa. Thanks to centuries of exchange between neighboring nations, many words and expressions had stayed more or less the same. I wondered whether there might not be analogies between the speech of old, stable societies, nurtured by the sea, and the terns.

Was human speech a conscious, cultural projection, while the cries and communication of birds had an entirely different origin? Perhaps they were closer than that. After all, degrees of geographical isolation have shaped human speech. Like the terns, we had our islands, our racial and community inheritance. Each species of tern had its own voice and vocabulary, its own way of transmitting messages, and at least, even if they failed to change, their inner content might be more elaborate than we knew.

When I came back to Cape Cod and walked out over the

marsh again, I decided to listen a little harder, or listen while I watched. I heard them, all over again, generating excitement with their crying. I heard "Kip-kip" as they landed, postured, or flew away. "Ahrk!" was the call of birds that chased each other, or at times a "Chatta-chatta!" I heard Roseate Terns, apparently in alarm, give an almost crow-like "Rrahnk" or "Ahnk," and they made shrill and squeaky calls on other occasions, sometimes sounding a little like songbirds. And there were "Keearhs" and "Chivees" and many other cries, in the air, on the ground, half notes, whole notes, mutterings, garglings, exclamations.

At least to begin with, though I could hear and feel some coordination between a cry and the action that accompanied it, I could not specify the intent. In fact their cries do not seem to anticipate, assess, or elaborate on what a bird is doing, but are simply part of it. Sound accompanies impulse and gesture. But calls are also signals, as anyone who has heard a trumpeting flock of Canada Geese must know. When a tern switched from one call to another— "Keearr," say, followed by "Kip-kip"—I supposed, without precisely knowing what was going on, that it was some change in mood or intent to another, such as "I am taking off, an intruder is coming." But after I heard both calls during courtship flights, when they seemed to be interchangeable, I concluded that the question was one of mutual response rather than of specific intention.

Common Terns changing over at the nest seemed to "talk" to each other. The female would beg rapidly at first, with "Ki-ki-ki-ki," after which her mate might or might not bring her a fish. They would both sound a fairly low "Keeyer." The male would address her with a rapid "Korr-korr-korr-korr-korr," which could change into a croupy, gargling "Kuh-kuh-kuh-kuh." The sounds he made were hoarse and watery, as though coming from somewhere down in a pipe, and could change to a remarkable degree. I heard one bird leaving its replacement behind on the nest, making a slight "Tik-tik" of a sound as it plucked at some grass, and then a louder "Tik-tik-tik-tik" as it flew away.

A Common Tern flying at an intruder, or threatening to do so, first gives a rough, rattling note of warning, which sounds like "Eeurrh," followed by a rapid "Kuta-kuta-kuta-kuta," or so I thought; but since I was listening carefully when I first heard it and later came up with "Ka-ka-ka-ka," I was none too confident of my human ear as a transcriber of bird calls. A tern that seemed really angry and excited would end these whipped-out cries with a wild "Ahk!" or "Ahrk!"—which I have also seen written down as "Kaarrr!" I can only say, each to his ear, or perhaps you to your larynx and the tern to its syrinx, from which all these sounds come.

Each species of tern has its own voice, though some of their individual calls may sound very similar. J. M. Cullen says that Arctic and Common Terns "have an almost identical vocabulary," and that with a few exceptions their calls are hardly distinguishable. But when I first heard Arctic Terns I thought the quality of the sound was quite different from that of the Commons. I find the difference hard to describe. Perhaps their dominant calls were smoother, more even, and at the same time more shrill. The "Tika-tika-tika" call heard in both species is "pickier" in the Arctic. If it is a common language, the way it is spoken is distinct in the two species.

Helen Hays, director of the research center at Great Gull Island, pointed out to me that if you transcribe it without the customary K, the call of a male Common

Tern trying to lead a female down to the ground is a nasal, almost growling "Ayhnurr-ahn-ahn-ahn." Some of the calls of this species sound both strident and silvery, others harsh and deep, and still others seem to be little more than casual, absentminded note takings, which may verge abruptly into wild excitement. A bird flying by itself with a fish may utter a noncommittal "Ketuh-ketuh," whereas one being furiously chased by others intent on robbing it will give a high, hysterical "Kekearr!" in its distress. An abrupt "K-kaah" may accompany a brief flurry with another bird passing in flight. Possible causes of excitement or alarm often turn into reality in the life of terns, and their cries slur from one to another accordingly, mounting from low to high.

As I listened, terns often sounded as though they were making announcements about presentations, departures or arrivals, things to fly away from, things to be attacked. It was all part of the formality of their behavior. They seemed to say, "I have something" (such as a fish), or, "Move over," or "Give"—statements of immediacy. They had their own cries with respect to trangressors of order in their own ranks, and toward outsiders. Without being able to employ conscious meaning in our sense, they still meant like mad in their own terms, as far as I could tell.

I never felt that either their behavior or their communication, limited though it might be, could be satisfactorily accounted for through a study of reflexes, releasers, and so on. This kind of jargon has its uses, but it can also confine us to the terms of an age whose "releaser mechanisms" are making us jump like robots hundreds of thousands of miles into space, or simply across the room so as to turn down the commercials. On the other hand, it may not be much better to reduce a tern's entire expression to "Keearr," or a robin to "Cheerup." Bird calls do not translate very well into any equivalent in human speech, or even into musical notation. It also seems likely that we do not even hear them half the time.

In his study of bird song, which he also calls vocalization, Crawford Greenwalt emphasizes that the performance of birds is related to their organic ability to discriminate. In other words, they are able to learn complex phrases and sounds, and to remember them. The sounds they produce by means of the syrinx ". . . can be modulated, either in frequency, or in amplitude, or more usually in both, with extraordinary rapidity, so rapidly in fact that human ears cannot perceive the modulations as such, receiving instead an impression of notes of varying quality and timbre." Furthermore, birds evidently hear these modulations as such, so that individuals of the same species can recognize one another by vocal subtleties that are lost to the human ear. The information content in even the simplest songs must be enormous.

It seemed to me that I could not judge this non-human life by the limitations of a language I was unable to understand, and could only half hear; all I could do was to confess the limitations of my own senses, and try to start from there. But what I did make out from listening to the terns' harsh, reedy, or watery cries were gradations in pitch and emphasis that came from the intensity of their feelings. Their calls, from which I might be able to distinguish a number that apparently denoted more or less the same thing, were part of an elaborate continuity of response.

Niko Tinbergen in *The Herring Gull's World* says, "One often gets the impression that birds call when they are strongly activated by an internal urge, and yet cannot satisfy that urge by performing the activities to which it drives them." Even so, continued communication was something I was as much aware of as individual frustration. All of these intense birds, potentially ready to react at any time in response to another's cry, are socially related to a degree that they can fly off in a body, at times with a lot of noise, or at others in eerie silence.

Away from their nesting island, during the non-breeding season, they behave as part of a flock rather than as individuals pairing up and protecting their own nests. Nevertheless, there is a latent unity on the nesting territory as well, which shows not only in outflights but a constant mutual awareness. Each cry, attitude, or gesture from any one bird can radiate out to others, in the immediate vicinity, or throughout the whole colony. This awareness—a crowd on the alert—implies a tribal tyranny of the species over the individual. Survival is hardly democratic.

Still this organic unity is wonderfully tuned. The birds respond to each other nervously, but also with a kind of fierce desire. I kept moving toward them, listening to them, not as if they were entirely alien factors, but as if we had a collateral relationship whose depths were beyond conscious knowledge. Their behavior, in fish flights, in aggressive flurries, in coaxing each other, coaxed my feelings too. I thought of all the attempted approaches and compulsive retreats I, and everyone else I knew, had experienced as part of our deep community. We did not do it out of a vacuum of unilateral effort. We responded in terms of the authority of life on earth. My own awareness was possessed by its ceremonials.

9

Eggs and Their Defenders

A morning after heavy rain. Fog hid the low dunes in the distance. The salt marsh was springy underfoot, the sharp grasses scraping my bare feet. A Common Tern came into sight, swinging by me to dip, turn, and drop over a marsh pool. Trying to catch its food, it hovered, paused, and twisted, in a fine test of skill that temporarily failed. So it went beating off again, in its quick and limber style, to scan another fishing place.

Spring green from the stalks of the cordgrass now covered the humps and shoulders of the marsh along its inlets and ditches, and over the flat peaty levels little nubbins of luminous green saltwort were thrusting upward. Semipalmated sandpipers rose up and flitted away as I came on, crying out in trilling whispers, and through the fog I could hear the winding, concentrated sound of the ternery, like some great hive. As I came closer, the scouts on the perimeter started to cry out and then attack. I heard the dry "Raack!" of a Roseate overhead, and a Common flew at me with "Kukukuku-*kak!*" Walking slowly through the nesting area, watching my feet, but steadily, so as not to keep the birds too long in the air, I found many nests with eggs in them. Common Terns lay two or three as a rule, and the Roseates lay one and sometimes two. I found the nests of the latter in a heavier growth of beach grass, or in hollows between clumps of dusty miller, beach heather, or beach pea.

These eggs were what all that fury of trying led to. I could not see one now, here or in a single sparrow's nest in some inland thicket, without thinking of what an achievement they were, apex of the wild, the precious, the expendable. All the wild bird eggs I have ever seen are wonderfully subtle in their reflection of the ground that receives them. Terns' eggs are no exception; their speckled shells are of rock and sky and summer sands and of shadows woven by the grass. They are marked by atmospheres; they lie like pebbles and stones burnished by sunlight.

Most eggs, though they may look at first glance like any others, are recognizable according to the species. A Roseate's egg is likely to be paler than that of a Common, slightly more pointed, and with finer, less blotchy speckles and spots, which tend to form a ring at one end. The eggs of the Sandwich Tern are usually very pale in color, as the chicks will be, sometimes a creamy white, with black markings like some still undeciphered calligraphy. They are larger than those of Common or Roseate Terns and somewhat more conical in shape.

On the other hand, I believe that there is no really reliable way of distinguishing between the eggs of Common and Arctic Terns, though there may seem to be enough of a difference here and there to encourage a connoisseur to keep on trying to prove it. Coloring, incidentally, may vary with locality. I have heard that in the high-Arctic regions of Greenland, Arctic Terns lay eggs that are considerably darker than in the more southerly parts of the country.

Eggs in the same nest may vary a great deal. One might be a pale blue, or bluish-green, while the one next to it is a cloudy brown. The same female, incidentally (and this is also true of other birds such as Oystercatchers), will come back year after year to the same site and lay eggs with the same variations in color. Chicks too can be quite different in color, at least before they are feathered out. I saw two baby Least Terns in the same nest, with down that was grayish in one and a light nut-brown in the other.

Learning to distinguish eggs may not seem a matter of monumental importance, but the more I find the human world around me occupying all territory on its own terms, the more such specks, shapes, and markings mean to me. They are earth's signatures. They are an example, in the face of uniformity, of how life can never be followed in terms of anything but unmatched creation. How fresh all its inventions are, after millions of years! Our vision requires this detail.

The color of the egg may be related to the behavior of the bird. The whitish eggs of the Sandwich Tern, and to a lesser degree those of the Roseate, are more conspicuous than those of Arctic, Common, and Least Terns. This is partly compensated for by the habit of Sandwich Terns of nesting in dense colonies, as Roseates often do where they are more numerous. Sandwich Terns also defecate around their nests instead of walking away from them as a Common Tern will do. This makes the nests easier to see; nor do they carry broken eggshells away. All this would seem to heighten the danger from predators, but Sandwich Terns do not leave their nests when a hawk or a gull flies over, but stay where they are. The Arctic and Common species have a different form of protection. Their nests are scattered rather than concentrated, so the birds fly up and distract intruders by attacking them, while the uncovered eggs are well camouflaged, and so are the chicks.

So the egg lies exposed, bare but blended in, in the way of each passing foot or hand, each skunk or rat, of gulls and of storm waves. Yet it represents a trust of a kind, which men may share with terns. Least Terns often lay their eggs just above the reach of the tides. Do we not also, in our unconscious, trust the regularity and forbearance of tides that might inundate us?

In my periodic visits, I saw how fog and rain curtailed mating and fishing flights, and there was reason to think egg-laying was held up too. When the daily egg count fell off, someone on Great Gull Island had said, "Perhaps they sense bad weather coming on." When a few terns were found to have laid eggs where they were roosting on rocks at the fringes of the nesting area, rather than on the nests themselves, it was guessed that thunder and lightning the night before had unnerved them to that extent. It was generally agreed that fine weather encouraged the egg-laying and bad weather discouraged it. The terns were certainly as volatile as the weather, and had an elemental relationship with it.

After the eggs are laid they are incubated continuously except when an intruder comes to the ternery, or a panic occurs, or when the birds leave their nests to defecate. Males and females share to some extent in sitting on the eggs, though the females spend more time at it than the males. When a female has finished laying eggs and begins incubating them, it is a period when she needs to regain her strength, and for some days she is fed at the nest by her mate. This is a critical period for her, and for the future of the nest, and it goes better with a good provider.

Incubation, by the way, is not a matter just of keeping eggs warm but also of keeping them cool. Too long an exposure to hot summer sun will destroy the embryo. The minimum incubation period for the egg of a Common Tern seems to be about twenty-one days, but repeated or sporadic disturbance may lengthen the period. The average is likely to be between twenty-four and twenty-six days.

Changing over at the nest has its ceremonial aspects. When a male brings a fish to a female, they posture, bow and bend, inclining heads and necks upward at various angles. When he has no fish, she is likely to beg for it. They are both restless in each other's presence and toward the need for continuous incubating of the eggs. After the male begins to share in the nest sitting, the two change over with no particular regularity. A male may sit on the nest for hours or only minutes. One of a pair may fly in, prompting its mate to leave the nest, but if the first does not settle in and start brooding right away the other will often come back again.

Before it leaves them, a bird that has been sitting on eggs often indulges in preening gestures, sometimes plucking at grass and sticks around the nest as well, tossing them over its shoulder or passing them along its feathers. This has been interpreted as showing a conflict between a strong desire to brood the eggs along with a contrary urge to desert them. As a result of this picking and strewing around of grass and sticks, a nest scrape will gather quite a good deal of material around it which the birds never put there intentionally.

There is a fussiness, with much adjusting, when a tern

settles down on its eggs in the nest. It will often make a motion of tucking or nudging them under its ventral feathers, and experiment shows that it will do this even when the eggs have been removed. Apparently the position of an egg in the nest is very important to them. Gulls and terns are not averse to sitting on substitute eggs made of wood or plastic, and they do not seem to be able to tell the difference at first, but the exact position of the eggs seems very important.

In a film of nesting Fairy Terns on an island in the Indian Ocean, I saw at least one reason why the birds themselves did not dislodge their eggs from their precarious perches. A Fairy Tern coming back to incubate its one egg, which sat out on a bare and narrow branch, moved up and over it with natural lightness and instinctive care, hardly touching the egg until it settled down on top of it.

Watching the Common Terns at their nests was a great pleasure to me. I listened to their croupy, velvety talk. I watched them posture when they got off the nest or approached it, and heard them cry to one another when they flew in. And when a tern exchanged places with its mate and settled down on the eggs, adjusting its pure gray feathers, the tail cross forked behind it, its gestures seemed as intent and protective as any I have ever seen.

One morning I had been lying in the hollow behind a low dune watching the nests on the edge of the territory, and when I got up, a few males started after me, with screams of alarm and outrage. So I retreated until I was far enough away to satisfy them.

Some individual terns are more militant than others. There was one at Great Gull Island that used to tear around a corner to attack any visitor or member of the staff who showed up, and some found it downright exasperating. To some extent familiarity breeds contempt in terns. The aggressiveness in some of them became almost automatic with people whose rounds they had become accustomed to.

When you watch them long enough, terns show that they are more than just birds of a feather. Some are clearly devoted to the duties of bringing in fish to a mate, sitting on a nest, or feeding chicks, and others do only a mediocre job. Robbers, aggressors, lovers—and I use the term advisedly—home-builders, or fishermen, all bring varying degrees of attention to their roles.

A great deal is usually made of territory when tern behavior is discussed, but aggressiveness is not always limited by home boundaries. A friend of mine and his boy were out in a rowboat on a Cape Cod pond, where no terns were nesting within miles, and one dove down and pecked the boy on the back of his head. Of course, this bird may have had experience with human beings before and was merely acting on it. On the other hand, such odd behavior might only mean that it was the season to attack.

Once I caught sight of a seal swimming not far offshore, and almost simultaneously all the terns along that part of the shoreline flew up and out over the water, and then back down again, posturing and crying. I could not imagine that a harbor seal represented any kind of a menace, as an owl or a rat would have, but perhaps the terns recognized any swimming mammal as a potential enemy. I supposed their reaction was innate. They did not behave in the same way toward a boat.

On Great Gull Island, I was told of another occasion when terns in still larger numbers had made a concentrated attack on a seal. It was later in the season after many of the birds had raised their chicks, and their flocking tendencies were stronger. After a few sighted the animal and rose into the air, many followed, fairly swarming out after the seal, circling over it and individually diving out of the flock very much as they do when fishing. They alternated in diving at its head and then withdrawing, until it swam out to a distance that satisfied them.

Herring and Black-backed Gulls can be roosting on the edge of a ternery, on dunes or offshore rocks, and not arouse the colony at all; but if a gull flies over the territory, transgressing a boundary that the terns understand, they will attack and drive it off.

Females as well as males act aggressively. They all do, including chicks at an early age, though the adult males go at it with the greatest intensity. Unless forewarned, people attacked by terns for the first time often don't know how to react.

The Farne Islands were visited by boatloads of visitors when the tide was favorable. The warden told me while I was there that some schoolchildren who had seen Alfred Hitchcock's film *The Birds* on television had been very apprehensive about being attacked by savage terns when they arrived on the island where they nested. In that nervous frame of mind perhaps, one small boy had an encounter with an Arctic Tern, whose nest was quite close to the roped-off path that led up from the water. I saw the fierce little grayish, black-capped bird with blood-red bill as it began to swoop back and forth just above his head, which had a dark blue, schoolboy's cap of its own. The boy was startled at first, and ready to run, but then valor won out. He suddenly put his fists up and began to duck and dance as if he was in a boxing ring, all the while yelling loud threats. Both parties disengaged shortly after that, with their honor intact.

A biography of Rose Fitzgerald Kennedy tells how she and her father, the noted Boston politician "Honey Fitz," were once strolling on the beach and were attacked by a flock of terns, which must have had nests not far away. "Honey Fitz" was outraged by the arbitrary pests and appealed for assistance to the selectmen of the town of Hyannis. They in turn brought in the local conservation officer, who tried to scare off the birds by firing blanks at them, only to have the birds swoop away and come back again, fearlessly and repeatedly. The officer, or possibly an enlightened game warden, suggested to a state office that the birds be shot; luckily, there were federal laws against that. Then, apparently, the redoubtable mayor threatened to appeal directly to the federal government.*

Our innocence of nature when translated into the uses of human power has frightening potentialities. Like some city or suburban children whose idea of the natural world comes from watching Tarzan on television, we can only expect something aggressive and dangerous from it, without knowing what that might be. We are curiously hidden from the reality of nature, even when a real robin is outside singing on a real tree. Our temptation, with this nearly mythical bias, is overwhelming force, guaranteed self-protection.

I am unsure, a great deal of the time, of what is meant by the term "aggression." Nature's genius lies in containing it rather than concentrating on it. Nor would it seem that most of the human race know what to make of aggression either; we are likely to overreact when we meet it in one another, we choke on our own restraint when we feel it in

* Gail Cameron, *Rose* (New York: G. P. Putnam's Sons, 1971).

ourselves, and we try to crucify it when we see it in non-human lives. We call out the army to deploy their helicopters against a mosquito, and wolves become the victims of our own myths about their depravity. When we become deluded enough to think that nature itself is the real pest, we start turning the bombs and poisons against ourselves.

Since terns are creatures of impulse, it is hard to analyze their actions at any given moment. And, in a sense, they may escape behavioral analysis, simply because of the rhythmic latitude in their ways. Ritual may be set, habits constrictive, but an observer is often unable to predict their behavior simply on the basis of set patterns. The options in their lives are at times invisible, not employed when expected. After all, it is a marvelously intricate depth of life, world, and weather to which they are tuned. The why or when of their outflights is an example of this, and also their habit of stealing from one another.

Their "robbing," as it is termed, is not uniform at all; it may be entirely absent in some colonies, it may occur randomly in others, or suddenly become a widespread local habit. As far as I can find out, robbing between adults occurs when a colony is under exceptional stress, such as a failure in the food supply. In recent years the terns at Plymouth, Massachusetts, which had been suffering from a reduced supply of fish in nearby waters, took to piracy, as some ornithologists have called it. A certain number of parents seemed to get most of the food for their chicks this way.

Stray individuals may become pirates too, and are often very skillful at their trade. In Norfolk, England, I saw a Roseate Tern flying rapidly and low, back and forth over a patch of ground where there were a few nests. Then it began to dip up and down, a little the way terns do when they are trying to catch a flying insect high in the air; and suddenly, quicker than the eye could follow, it snatched a fish from the bill of a Common Tern that was carrying it down to its nest. The victim never had the chance to duck at all but stopped in mid-flight, looking absolutely stunned by the disappearance of its fish.

Since we all make value judgments on the basis of personal feelings, aggressiveness in terns might be something to admire, "the brave little birds," or to detest. I have heard both reactions. Whether or not a man likes terns, however, he cannot help being struck by the vehement nature with which creation has endowed them. They are almost continually quarrelsome, or about to be. The distinctions they make between friend and enemy seem none too clear. In their nervous agitation they appear to have very little leeway; they are narrow and self-concentrated, readily alarmed, immediately dependent on outer stimulus. Perhaps they fear the unknown, but with a fear I would not know how to define. Their characteristics have vaguely human parallels, though it is probably not useful to look for direct ones where they cannot exist.

All the same, they had my hopes and sympathy with them in their constant drive to raise a family in the face of continual danger, and their intensely close relationship with the influences around them led me on. They defended life, and the practice never ceased.

10

Basic Skill

In June while they were incubating eggs, and after the middle of the month, brooding chicks, there was no letup in the feeling of urgency in the colony, in fact it increased. The birds were always at work, in motion, or waiting for a change in motion. Even with a majority on their nests, aerial courtship was still going on. I remember seeing terns racing together, rising up toward the clouds above the sea, and thinking not only what an accomplished art they were engaged in but how astonishing it was. For an animal so held to the ground by gravity that he could scarcely fall without hurting himself, this display of bonding and intense feeling hundreds of feet in the air seemed, for a moment, almost miraculous.

I was always aware of a certain number of birds going back and forth on fishing expeditions. They flew out long and low over the water, skipping forward, dipping their bills into the surface quite often, and then were lost to sight. When they returned, they raced by, often chased furiously when they carried fish, showing every kind of ability to twist and dodge, to swoop down, swing, and lift up again.

A tern has narrow wings, which do not allow it to soar like a gull, but they are long and very maneuverable. The bird takes off quickly and then seems to use the sea airs not only with skill but pleasure. Terns can beat their way into the wind, plying it with an easy rowing motion, and then shift all of a sudden to the side and fling back downwind with an abandon that suggests they enjoy it.

Like so much in their behavior, their busyness and agitation on the territory was in part a function of their tendency to move away from it. Within a period of three months after the males had made their first scrapes, the whole process of egg-laying, incubating, brooding, and rearing chicks would be over, unless casualty stopped it earlier. As I had seen them migrate in, so I was always conscious that everything they did implied a departure. The chicks themselves had to grow at a furious rate so as to be ready for a journey toward distant coasts they had never seen before.

The voyages of the Arctic Tern are amazing, not only in terms of mileage. It travels from one end of the earth to the other and back and has time to raise a family in between. Its actions are so synchronized with global conditions that a season of rearing young either seems like some superbly machined adaptation or a dare taken in the face of impossibility.

I learned in Denmark that Arctic Terns breeding in the more southerly regions of Greenland—in other words, the low Arctic—arrived there by mid-May or a little later, and started laying eggs anywhere from the beginning to the end of June. They apparently left in late August. This is a breeding period only a little longer than for Commons and Roseates in temperate latitudes, though the young of the Arctics may not be able to linger, feeding on an autumn supply of fish, as long as the other species.

On the other hand, Artic Terns breeding in the high Arctic regions of Greenland, prevented by ice from migrating to their breeding grounds any earlier, did not start laying eggs until mid-June, or later—which seems to be true of Arctics nesting in the northwest territories of Canada. Since they left their high Arctic territories between mid-August and the beginning of September, when the ice closed in again, the time they had for incubating eggs and rearing young was short. Arctic Terns whose nests still contained eggs or chicks too late in the season had to abandon them. This kind of timing did not allow the young to grow in the arts of flying and fishing before they had to migrate. So they presumably followed the adults and continued to be fed at sea. It has been asserted also that young Arctic Terns take less time to learn to fly than Commons do. Even where they nested in temperate zones, Arctic Terns might have to incubate their eggs in a slightly shorter period than the Common Terns; and they might have to arrive a little later or leave a little earlier—all of which could be accounted for by the species' adaptation to a short summer in the Arctic. It is a tight schedule, and it reveals the exactions called for from these graceful birds, to an awesome extent; but how ready they are! In my mind's eye, I see them roosting on ice floes in the Canadian Arctic, during a night that hardly shows itself as anything but an hour or two of twilight. I see them floating and beating their way over to Europe, and skipping across open leads in the ice on another long day of light in the Antarctic. What surpasses this ability to comprise the earth, known and unknown, in your very being?

So a balance between arrival and departure is built into the actions of migratory terns from the start. Of course their behavior on their nesting grounds is quite different from what it is during the rest of the year, and it is worth pointing out that they spend more of their lives over the water than they do on land. There is always at least a potential pull in them away from their islands, if only because there is more safety by sea than by land.

I was always conscious of the innate ability in these birds to time their actions to a season, to be able to move away in the face of calamity, or to start in and nest again if they had to. On the other hand, to bow to limitations, there is just so much their native capabilities can manage, just so much the earth can supply them with. They may not be able to accommodate to wildly shifting food supplies, and the breeding islands themselves do not always hold out. A sandy island, a sand dune, a pebbly beach, or even an island made of rock may be subjected to violent storms or rising sea levels. Billingsgate Island in Cape Cod Bay, where substantial buildings stood in the recent past, simply disappeared. Normally, both nesting territories and the birds themselves are flexible enough so as to provide alternatives. The world of coastal seas is changeable; some of its islands may disappear, fish may come and go, but in the past at least, the environment has been consistent enough to supply seabirds with what they needed.

Years ago, I visited an island in Bull Bay, South Carolina, where Royal and Sandwich Terns and Brown Pelicans were nesting. (The Royal Tern is a warm-water bird, whose range on both sides of the American continent is restricted by the colder ocean currents. When these currents shift, the Royal Tern may extend or limit its range accordingly, as it follows certain kinds of warm-water fish.)

Out beyond the channeled marshes where an Oystercatcher wheeled by like a discus, and Snowy Egrets lifted up, classically graceful, the small island lay out in the shallow waters of the bay, behind a long barrier beach. We landed on a narrow strip of sand which encircled hummocks on higher ground where pelicans nested, and a center of marshland, where willets nested.

Each pair of pelicans had an area of about four square feet of nesting space. When I saw them, ponderously sitting, I thought first, "How distinguished they look," and then "How stupid and awkward!" This bird was one of nature's exotics, grotesque but well finished, with multicolored feathers, and an odd, downward hanging, pouched beak. It was made to look grave and strange, doubtless for grave and strange reasons. The white, chocolate, and cream, or sometimes yellow in their heads and necks, the grizzled brown on their backs and wings, contrasted with the beach and mist colors of the trim-bodied terns. When we got to within twelve or fifteen feet of their nests, they raised their heavy wings and took off silently, with quick, sure strokes; and anyone who has seen them gliding effortlessly along the surf line knows that they too have a rhythmic alliance with the sea.

The Royal Terns were big birds, as compared with a Common or a Roseate. They were ranked along the beach, a handsome company with distinctive black crests and orange bills, a ready, nervous, upward-looking way of carrying themselves, like a thoroughbred horse. "Brrahk!" they cried, as they took off elegantly into the air. Their wings had a longer, looser motion than those of the smaller Sandwich Terns that were flying farther down the beach. These two species often associate.

Because it was early in the season, the Royal Terns were not yet nesting, but I could see a few engaging in aerial courtship far overhead, and they had already made some bare scrapes in the sand. Later on, their eggs would be scattered across the beach like so many white stones. Both the Sandwich and Royal Terns nested closely and noisily together, in fairly compact groups. The waters around the island were only two or three feet deep and the tides were negligible, so that the nests close to the high-tide line were normally safe; but spring storms sometimes washed them out and the birds would have to start all over again. In this region the Royals laid only one egg, very rarely two, which does not necessarily indicate, as I once heard it suggested, a protective adaptation in the face of losses by spring storms over thousands of years. Other species lay small clutches, and the evidence seems to show that this relates to the shifting nature of the food supply, often scarce, and the competition for it. Also, Royal Terns feed their young for an unusually long period after they are hatched—up to seven months, in fact—while they are developing the skillful fishing techniques they will need to survive. Since this is exacting for the parents, there would seem to be a definite advantage in their not having too many chicks to take care of.

To share these watery territories involves special abilities. Each species of tern has its own manner of getting food. Roseates, with more streamlined, slightly less chunky bodies than the Commons, and with shorter wings, can plunge as much as a foot deeper into the water and so reach fish not available to the other. They can fly at a speed that has been estimated at fifty percent faster, and will go out directly miles over the water to dependable fishing grounds where they can catch fish such as sand launces. While a Common Tern will fly some distance for its food, it is often obliged to depend on a less reliable supply in shallower waters.

Sandwich Terns may fly even farther out than Roseates do. I am told that from a colony at Scolt Head in the English county of Norfolk, they go as far as Rice Bank for their food, a distance of thirty to forty miles. They can dive deep enough, incidentally, to almost totally immerse themselves, and stay under for several seconds, with the result that they can reach fish that frequent different levels from those reached by other terns. The Sooty and Noddy Terns of the tropics may travel still greater distances for the small squid and fish driven to the surface by tuna, the Brown Noddy as much as fifty miles and the Sooty several hundred. The Sooty Tern chicks are able to go without food for several days while their parents are absent, but the noddies, whose wider wings are less suited for long-distance travel and staying on the wing, have to return to the colony at night.

The matter of depth at which various sea animals occur is of critical importance to the terns, especially where an accustomed food supply gives out. Since the supply of fish was so poor at the Plymouth colony, the Common Terns nesting there had changed over to shrimp, which now made up about two-thirds of their diet. These were mainly a species of mud shrimp which the birds could reach only during the two or three hours while the tide was ebbing, and when they were at a level where it was not too deep to catch them. As a result, there was simply not enough food, and many chicks died of starvation; and, as I mentioned earlier, adults were forced into robbing from one another.

From the fish lying uneaten on the ground, you can get a rough idea of what the birds are catching during a given season, but not necessarily what the young are eating, since the rejected fish are the ones you see. On a tern island in Maine, I found young sea herring, alewives, cunners, and sticklebacks, even a little spiny-bodied sea robin; on Cape Cod, sand launces and silversides; on Great Gull Island, pipefish, anchovies, mackerel, and butterfish, among others. Terns along the more southerly reaches of the coast might pick up silversides, anchovies, menhaden, and other species. The kinds of fish to be found vary with the locality, and they vary as well in abundance and in the time they appear, from day to day and from week to week. Some years show a far greater number of species than others. Occasionally one kind of fish may leave a region altogether. The fry of hake were once abundant in the shallow waters off Nantucket Island, and provided a major part of the diet for terns breeding and fishing in that area; then they disappeared, and the birds had to switch to other food.

I wondered, in the light of the plundering of the fish supply over the continental shelf, the contamination of marine organisms by oil, chemical wastes, and even plastic, as well as the pollution, filling, and eradication of salt marshes, streams, and estuaries where fish were nurtured, whether the terns were not going to be even more restricted and threatened as time went on.

Since, with occasional exceptions, terns are "one-prey

feeders," catching only one fish at a time, they spend considerable time and energy doing it. Going after food for their young involves a keen degree of effort, which is both defined and frustrated by the fluctuating nature of the food supply.

Larger colonial birds such as kittiwakes and cormorants spend far less time getting their food. They feed their chicks by regurgitation, not having to fly miles out to catch and bring back a single fish. Each parent supplies enough to feed the entire brood when it returns from a fishing trip, with the result that the parents can alternate, sharing brooding and fishing equally. Parent terns, on the other hand, are often away together after their chicks are a few days old. A pair may spend anywhere from seventeen to nineteen hours a day on the business of getting food, which suggests that the terns might be close to a physical limit beyond which it would not be economical to feed on small fish. Exhaustion and starvation seem to hang beyond the nineteenth hour. That it gets done is a tribute to a tern's skill and continual intentness.

Terns have to keep scanning the water; they have to swerve quickly and dive with accuracy, in order to get their food when it appears. They have to take advantage of the brief appearance of fish, sometimes driven to the surface by larger predators; carried up by tidal currents; or drawn by changes in the temperature of the water, sometimes artificially effected. At the outfall of the power plant on the Cape Cod Canal, the water at the surface is from twenty to twenty-five degrees warmer than the water four feet beneath it. In this area of turbulence, where warm water interfaces with cold, small fish are momentarily shocked, turn belly up and are swept to the surface before they are able to right themselves. There they are tossed around like so many shiny slivers, an easy prey for gulls and terns.

Walking out over the sand flats, swimming off the beaches, or rowing offshore, I watched Common Terns traveling and fishing all summer long. They flew out and skimmed over the surface, they circled quickly, heeled over, plummeted in, then bobbed up to fly away, with or without a fish. They hovered and dove with dexterous fanning of feathers and twisting of wings, a pliant spreading, drawing in, and depressing of their tails. At times their intentness seemed extreme. One summer day, I watched a single tern from a rowboat in a Maine cove, winging from side to side over the water, dropping and lifting, so concentrated on the business of finding fish that it hardly noticed my boat, veering away suddenly just as it reached me.

Above all, on their tightrope of survival, the terns require skill. Whether or not a bird can catch fish, not tomorrow but now, for its mate, its young, itself, is the difference between life and death. A man may be able to move his operation from one offshore fishing ground to another and lose a few days, but this is a margin a tern cannot afford. In fact, the birds that are most successful are the ones that are able to switch from one kind of fish to another, not losing precious time on hunting for what has grown scarce.

To succeed, the individual hunter's senses must be highly refined. His arrow has to hit the target, and in this he may fail. A Common or an Arctic Tern may try and try again before it catches a fish, even when there is an abundance. The keenest eyesight, the most perfectly timed dive may not be enough. Besides, the fish themselves have eyes. They are watching the terns and have the means of descending quickly to avoid them. Apparently, however, the light grayish breast plumage of a tern may serve as camouflage so that fish are unable to see it readily. Cryptic coloration helps the predator as well as the prey.

One day I saw a small flock hovering over shallow waters that were running out swiftly over brown sands at the mouth of a tidal creek. They were dipping in and making easy, shallow dives. What were they finding? I walked over, looked down into bright water, and at first saw nothing. Then I caught sight of little flashing bursts of silver as tiny, almost transparent fish flickered against the brown sand. These were what the birds were after, while sunlight glared and made lacy patterns across the fast-moving current. It was a surprise to me that the terns could manage to catch anything at all. The refraction of light on water is extremely misleading, and a fish may be below where you think you see it. Those fast, glittering waters were a confusion to sight, with a motion that was intensely distracting. In fact, it may be somewhat distracting to terns too, since they appear to have more trouble fishing in rough weather.

I drew off again from the outlet of the creek, and after a while a few terns came back. They hovered into the wind, wings beating rapidly, and then, seeing a fish a little ahead of them, compensating I supposed for the angle of refraction, they pitched forward, twisting a little in flight as they dove, with wings closed or partly closed, depending on the depth at which the fish were swimming. I watched a skill that often failed, that could not fail, an art of life.

11

Hunger

Several days before a tern chick emerges from its egg, a "starring" can be seen on the shell; then later on a hole with a bill beginning to poke through, and in about a day after that the chick is hatched, waggling weakly, damp at first, though the down dries quickly. While the egg is pipping, the parents act in a nervous and uneasy way. Once the chick is finally hatched, the adult female is reluctant to leave the nest at all, even during an alarm, since chicks are at a very delicate and fragile stage of their existence.

If you have to walk through a ternery, especially at midday, it is best to go straight on without lingering. Not only are the eggs vulnerable, but newborn chicks are unable to regulate their own temperature and have to be brooded. If the parents are kept up in the air too long by disturbance, newborn chicks are in danger from the killing heat of the sun, not to mention a passing predator such as a gull.

It is all very well to see an egg as expendable, just

because all eggs are expendable, which is the common attitude in our exploitative society; but I had begun to change my feelings about it. I had stepped on one soon to hatch, when I wasn't paying enough attention, and at this near stage of life and awareness, such carelessness was an act of murder. So I approached the nests and walked among them with the greatest care, trying, though my feet were too big and my actions clumsy, to step like a cat in the dark.

It was a hot day late in June. The leaves of the beach pea were folded over, and the beach grasses, gently switching, glistened with light, out where I could hear the gush and stir and backfalling of the waves. Terns sat on their nests panting in the heat. I saw one male bird fly in and try to deliver to its two- or three-day-old chick a fish that was much too big and slippery to manage. After gaping and reaching forward in a futile way toward the food, held in its parent's bill, the chick could not pick it up, and the parent gave no further help but flew away, to return later with another offering that proved to be a better size. Meanwhile the female sitting on the nest had picked the fish out of the sand and eaten it herself.

This sequence occurs fairly often, since a male Common Tern begins to bring in fish to a chick from a half an hour to an hour after it has hatched. He may also partly feed the female at this stage. At first the fish he brings in may be too big for the chick, as if he was not able to discriminate between what it needs and what his mate requires. But the male usually learns to adjust the size he catches, and a great deal depends on it. If he does not, the chick might very well die of starvation. These early days and hours of feeding are vital. For a starving chick, there is no second chance.

Such species as the Sandwich and the Roseate Terns have access to a more dependable supply of fish, in deeper waters, and they seem to be more selective than the Commons when it comes to feeding a newly hatched chick. They start with fish of a manageable size, and then bring in larger ones as the chick grows. The Common Tern is more random about it, sometimes producing a small minnow or pipefish, bits of shrimp or crab larvae, even insects, and then returns with a fairly large silversides or sand eel later on. The reason dead fish are so often found in a ternery is that the chicks cannot swallow them down. The younger they are, the harder time they have in picking up a fish that has been dropped on the ground, though the parents often try to help.

The little fawn chicks are cryptically colored, like the eggs they came from. The markings on their little bodies, with lines and patches like bits of light debris on a beach, tend to draw your eyes away from them.

"I am not here," says the chick, cast out onto a hungry planet.

From the beginning, the chick crouches down in the nest whenever it is frightened. After a few days, it has grown enough to be able to move a short distance away from its nest when disturbed and to return to it. As it grows still older and larger, able to scuttle and run, it finds nearby hiding places in grasses, seaweed, beach heather, or rocky crevices, all of which give better cover than the original nest; and it is here that the adults now go to feed them.

The fact that baby Least Terns move off to the shelter of nearby hollows along the coastal beaches where they were born has become a source of danger to them, because such hollows may have been formed by beach-buggy tracks. The innate adult tendency to avoid the land also shows itself in the chick. In terneries that are located above a beach, half-grown birds, and sometimes much younger chicks, will occasionally hurry off toward the water after being seriously disturbed. In Denmark, I saw a chick run across the beach and take to the water after a family and a dog had routed it out from its hiding place in the grass, though I don't believe they knew it was there, or the dog would have chased it. It swam fairly readily, though tidal currents were taking it off parallel to the shore. I could only hope it would escape being gobbled up by a passing Herring Gull.

Terns float in the water and bathe in it for brief periods. I have often seen small flocks of them splashing in the sea, then moving on after a few seconds to another spot, where I could see their heads ducking in and their wings beating as they bathed. But they are poor swimmers; their feet are too small to propel them efficiently for long, and prolonged immersion will drown them. Walking over rough ground can also cause them some difficulty. On Great Gull Island I noticed that Common Terns nesting between stones and boulders found it slippery and tippy going as they went back and forth to their nests. Their toes turned up slightly and they walked on the flat webs; their wings did most of the maneuvering.

From the time I first saw an egg chipped by the living thing inside it, then watched the chick emerging, I felt drawn to another kind of urgency in the colony. It was being repeopled by its ardent parents. The young were out on the world, and everything centered on their need to be protected and fed. I was aware, all the time, of the parents on their fishing expeditions between the island and offshore waters. I also saw how intensely the nests were defended. When a stranger landed too close to a bird that was brooding its new chicks, it was immediately threatened with attack. As the chicks grew, moving out to new hiding places, or simply favored spots where they waited to be fed, the parents defended them there, so the territory became less a specific piece of ground than the area around the young. Chicks began early to move out and enlarge their world. It was surprising too how soon they began to take on some of the scrappy character of their tribe. As the days went by and they kept on growing, they became increasingly militant—though in a somewhat erratic way—toward other chicks and adult strangers. All kinds of fierce attacks and quick withdrawals were in those little beings.

I watched a three- or four-day-old chick as it hid under a bit of driftwood, a foot or so away from its nest, after having been disturbed. When one of its parents returned, it came out and scuttled back again to the nest. The adult, which from past observation I guessed to be the female, turned toward the little one, stretching her wings, shivering and fluffing up her feathers, and then took it under her protection, cloaking it in a classic way, wings down and held out slightly to the side, tail feathers crossed behind her body. I felt sure this parent knew her chick.

On an island with hummocks, hollows, driftwood, thatch flung in by storms, with its growth of grass and beach plants, the birds and their nests are so spaced that you can understand how chicks could be identified, at least in terms of location. Each yard has its individuality. But when the chicks begin to move away, sometimes numbered in the hundreds or more, you wonder how it is possible for each one to be recognized. I suspect that the sight of thousands of Sooty Tern chicks on a nearly featureless tropical beach, each one known and fed by its parents, might seem even more remarkable. Yet place leads to place, life to life, knowing to knowing. Such recognition of child by parent does not surprise us in the human race. Why should it be surprising in birds? It keeps our mutual earth from anarchy.

During their first three or four days, chicks are continually brooded by their parents, with the female taking the larger share, and this seems to be the period when recognition starts. After about five days, when both parents may be off fishing instead of on the nest, they and their chicks will have learned each other's voices. The petulant cries of their offspring appear to stimulate the adults to feed them when they return. As a matter of fact, when the chicks are no longer in their original nest, it may indeed take their parents a while to find them. The chicks seem to have to come out and beg in order to be recognized.

I saw one parent fly in with a fish to a nest from which a chick had wandered some distance, and the adult did not seem to know where to look, or perhaps it was listening for a begging cry that failed to respond to its own call. In any case, it ended up by eating the fish itself. As it flies in, a parent Common Tern cries out with some special intonation of "Keearr" or "Keearree," meaning, perhaps, "Here's a fish." The chicks normally start up from sleeping or just digesting in the sun to beg frantically, with rapid, repetitious cries. Voice appears to play a strong part in recognition, since chicks react to hearing a parent when they are hidden from its view or when their eyes are closed. Since at a very early age they sometimes beg from adults that are not their parents, it may be that recognition develops and grows stronger after the chicks are a week or two old. Nevertheless, with different degrees of attention to the work, the chicks were found, they were fed, they were protected; and there was a quality of tenderness as well as mere driven necessity that characterized a parent's behavior toward its chicks, the tenderness that attaches the knower and the known.

While two birds were at the nest, feeding or brooding the chicks, changing places, or standing together, their vocalizing was like family talk. Their various gargling and almost warbling notes sounded as if they were working out problems together.

One parent tern would be brooding on the nest when its mate flew in, prior to a changeover, to peer under the other's wing, solicitously poking at the chick. As the first bird started to move off the nest, its mate then touched its bill to the young one's beak, as if to say, "Let's see how hungry you are," or, perhaps, "Who are you? How do you react?" I felt that there might be a profound domestic tale of terns to be put together out of countless minor incidents like that. Other demands and distractions took me away too soon. Chance acquaintance is never enough.

From the start, when a chick is able to utter only a thin squeak, holding out the tiny stumps that will be its wings, quivering, and soon, fairly hopping with hunger, it acts like the personification of a life demand in all the terns. The "Ki-ki-ki-ki-ki" or "Gli-gli-gli-gli-gli" of its begging are beginner's notes in the practice of existence. In a couple of weeks they will have become something like, "Argh-argh-argh-argh-argh" or "Aggh-aggh-aggh-aggh-aggh," which give way to a more varied range of cries as the birds grow older, resembling the "Keearr" of an adult. A hungry chick with its rattling voice often struts, jumps, and dances in the open like some antic, wayward child in a rage.

It seems likely that a shortage of food causes chicks to try and rob each other, or to move angrily against other chicks whether they have fish or not, and makes their begging even more frantic. Occasionally a young tern, feathered out enough to fly around by itself, but not old enough to have learned how to fish, will desert its home territory for some other, more distant area where chicks are being fed. There it will wait around until adults come in with food and then try and dash in to intercept it before it reaches its rightful owners. The one I watched was doing fairly well. I did not know whether this robbing habit would result in a young tern's having greater skill and initiative or would simply cut down on its food supply. Perhaps neither is the case and the bird simply gets away with it; and of course it may have had the habit forced upon it as a result of being deserted by its parents.

Hunger and a chick are synonymous. Listening to their begging, watching them come out from under a parent's wing so as to have more space to swallow a fish, jerking their heads and gulping hard as it went down, I thought, "I want! I want!" must be the most fundamental cry in all the world.

The appetite and capacity of a chick in its first few days are amazing. Those fish that it is able to swallow and not drop on the ground sometimes make it look like a man trying to get down a steak one-third his size. An adult presenting food to its young will hold a fish in its bill close to the head, so that a chick receives it that way. Occasionally the young gag and choke when they try to eat a fish tail first; as far as I know, it cannot be done. The chick first pecks toward the food as the parent holds it, then grabs and pulls at it, starting to swallow by jerking its head back. This pink-beaked, gaping, downy ball of expectancy makes frantic efforts to swallow anything it starts to get down. A chick may be seen with the head and half the body of a fish in the process of being swallowed while the tail is left hanging outside. Complete consumption of a fish small enough to swallow whole might take the chick no more than about twenty minutes.

Even an average requirement in tern young of a few ounces of fish a day would add up to a good many pounds by the time it was fledged. I have seen no statistics bearing on it, but I would guess that if you multiplied one chick's consumption by a thousand, more or less, depending on the size of the colony, the overall food requirement could be measured by the ton.

The biggest chick in a Common Tern's nest is very likely to get more food than its brothers and sisters, since it is more capable of grabbing a fish and swallowing at least a part of it when offered. Some adults may work harder at bringing in meals than others, but if there is a good supply of fish offshore, the amount fed to the chicks in any given nest seems to average out and they are equally nourished. Under certain conditions, though, one chick may be fed less than the others and be stunted or starved in the process. The feeding tempo might be interrupted, for example, if the parents took longer than usual to get fish, perhaps because of several stormy days. In that event, the largest nestling might be fed to the neglect of a smaller one. Of course, the size of fish brought in varies considerably with the kind available, not only from day to day and week to week, but also from one year to the next.

One morning I concentrated on the feeding routine for a nest in which there was a pair of chicks, four or five days old, one a little larger than the other. The larger chick was fed a sizeable fish at 10:30 A.M. and the other got nothing. At 11:40 a parent brought in another good-sized fish, which the smaller one took, only to have it grabbed away by its nest mate. At 11:58 the smaller one took a medium-sized fish, perhaps because its sister or brother was stuffed and lacked interest. Then, at 12:48 P.M., a bigger fish was brought in and offered to the smaller chick, but the larger one snatched it away again.

At 1:12 P.M., just before I left, the smaller chick was offered some bits of food which I couldn't recognize from a distance and promptly swallowed them. I never learned whether the pair was successfully reared or not, one of the minor frustrations of trying to learn something through occasional observation. I would like to have followed any of them to see them through; it seemed to me that they offered enough. It was a deep sea feeling I once had about alewives, but perhaps being left behind is part of the need to follow. The true nature of variety is always out of reach.

The rapacity of chicks is vital to them and their species. For a creature that is able to fly by the time it reaches thirty days, more or less, the imperative is never to stop growing. The physical and nervous crises this would entail for human beings if they grew at a commensurate rate does not bear thinking about. In the chicks change was visible from day to day. With my ear next to them all the while, I might have heard them rustling like growing corn on a summer's night.

During its first three days of existence, a chick doubles its weight, and in four more days doubles it again, and again in about eleven days after that. Then the curve begins to level off. In other words, the rate of feeding has to increase as the young continue to grow, although they consume relatively more to begin with and grow faster than they do later on.

Sometimes an adult does not move when its mate comes in with a fish, but goes on brooding the chicks. I saw a parent fly in with a pipefish, and then, not being able to deliver it—or at any rate having no chick emerge from a sheltering wing to beg for it—leave again, with an air of "What am I going to do with this?"

But while the young are very small, the shuttling back and forth with food goes on all day long. When a chick dropped a fish the parent would sometimes fly away; but just as often the fish would be picked up and presented again. I saw one parent watching with what looked to me like a patiently critical eye while its mate tried to reduce a still wriggling fish to manageable limpness, at the same time holding it before a single chick that was unable to get a grip on it. Finally the bird swallowed the fish itself and flew off to wash its bill by dipping it into the surface of the water. Occasionally an adult would fly off with a fish after a chick had dropped it, dip it in the water, and then come back to offer it once again. I have even seen a bird take a fish away from its mate and feed it to the chick, as if impatient.

I continually asked myself unanswerable questions. I still felt I had scarcely started, and felt little confidence about distinguishing between the sexes, guessing a bird's age, or sorting out what its actions signified. The period of chick-raising was another stage in intensity. I would have had to watch a single chick every day really to see its progress, a progress that was part of the colony as a whole as it raced through the tidal summer. Could I not usefully spend another lifetime on this formality of daily change?

Their own wild persistence was enough for me, whatever I thought I was looking at. God knows a tern chick is on fire with a spontaneity that needs no name. One of these babies, scarcely hatched, looking wobbly, incapable, and infirm, could literally bounce off the ground when a parent offered it a fish. Older chicks waiting to be fed hopped up and down and jumped around, begging and screeching with beaks agape, like noisy toys on springs. They let the world know who they were.

The handling, carrying, and offering of fish never stopped, but while chicks were being brooded or fed, and some eggs still incubated, crowds were roosting along the shelving peat and tidal sands below the island. Some of them dozed, with their bills neatly tucked inside their wings. I saw one preening, and suspected it was a male in the presence of a female: passing his head along his feathers with loose, slightly waggling motions, giving little shakes with his wing. When a new bird came in to land among the others it was greeted with upward stretching necks and bills.

On the nesting grounds, any tern coming in with a fish for its chicks could be chased immediately and furiously by other birds trying to take it away. The parent had to race, swoop, dash back and forth, until it gave its pursuers the slip and landed at the nest, or the place where its young were waiting. I saw one, coming in with a fast rush, another bird hard on its tail, drop the fish just as it reached its chick, which rushed forward and grabbed it. This kind of action excited all the birds in the vicinity. Parents stood over their young in protective attitudes, others cried out,

postured, or flew up. Even if the tern was not chased, its
arrival was received like an announcement, and not only by
its own chicks. Nearby adults not immediately engaged in
fishing or brooding young, many of them unmated, joined
in with even greater energy than the others. Such a tern
might open its bill and make a begging cry as if to say it
was only a week old itself and needed a handout. Not that
the terns were not natively ready to scream out, to chase
and be chased at all times, but even the *threat* of robbing
seemed to result in a show of latent excitement that pulsed
up and down on command.

I saw one chick begging fish from an adult that was
clearly not its parent and getting pecked on the head for it.
A chick that strays away from the ground where it is
defended by its parents, and goes too near other birds
brooding and feeding their young, is often pecked for the
transgression. When attacked, chicks crouch down sub-
missively—which is very much what they do when they
are about to rush out and peck at intruders themselves—
and this may be enough to make an adult tern cease and
desist. But the young can be pecked savagely, if seldom
killed. Death by exposure is more common.

There were many interchanges I could not interpret,
only record as I saw them. A male flew down and gave a
fish to a female that had been doing a nonstop begging act
on the ground. Another male came in crying, a fish in his
bill, and the adult he approached flew away as he arrived.
At times, though this could have been in part a result of my
ignorance as to what they were doing, I felt a certain
offhandedness, or even absentmindedness in their behavior.
They seemed to wait on each other's imperative demands.
Now and then a bird seemed to land almost forgetfully

with a fish and then it flew away again, or one would approach another and then break off as if lacking the stimulus to follow through whatever action it had started to perform.

Still, theirs was not a society so governed by impulse as to have lost its order and sense of purpose. They were always highly aware of the island and of their chosen territories on it. Rhythmic placement was always vital to them, from the eggs, to ritualistic positions at the nest or in courtship, to flying out over the sea. And throughout their mating and the rearing of the young, I felt a constant preoccupation in them with preemption and transgression of ground—place and feelings being set to right, and kept in balance. Running through all their actions was a mutual attentiveness.

Sometimes, childish phrases came to me while I was watching the terns, like the outbursts that often come from very young children, expressing delight or frustration; it seemed to fit their actions. I don't think so much of my own maturity as to have left such connections behind. For both of us, the game of life has its foundation in childhood, although an adult tern is closer to childhood, in time at least, than a grown man. All I could muster of facts and analysis, even with a degree of reason that a tern lacked, often seemed superficial to me, or on the top, like uprooted seaweed floating on the water. There was an unbridgeable distance between us, and at the same time, in the tern's simplicity I was conscious of a deeper level.

My visits to the island were, in a sense that I wanted to keep open, elemental journeys. I followed those hard, wild, formal exercises again and again, watching the pointed wings racing through the shimmering air. I met an unending interchange each time I started out again, surrounded by a great formal ease, wave wash, and tidal spin.

One morning the braided sands led off at low tide under a light fog, through which the sunlight had started to burn. The south wind cuffed away at sheets of low water, making feather patterns, purple and gray. I saw two Roseate Terns on the beach below the ternery acting out the primal style. As I saw her from behind, the female, head and neck stretched up proudly, had her wings parted like a bow reminding me of the shape of a horseshoe crab, or of a flounder, and the male, partly bent, held a fish, a glint of silver in the fog.

Food: the essential and the symbol. A fish of the tribe of fishes, having the color of reflecting waters: sunset yellow, copper, pink, and green; or steely blue; or intensely silver like a smelt, as tawny yellow and iridescent as a mackerel. There is no end to the reflections and exchanges of light and matter, as witnessed in their scales. In courtship a fish, not something to eat but a symbol, joins countless other ceremonies over the face of the globe.

It is said that courtship feeding, as ritualized in terns, has a value in maintaining the pair bond and presents a stereotyped pattern, though not more so, as behaviorists point out, than offering a ring to one's bride-to-be. In many ways, it resembles the presenting of food to the young. The male holds the fish, offers it, while the female begs. The fish flights, though much more elaborate than courting on the ground, derive from the same movements.

It is a strange thing, when you first become aware of it, to find in these birds the transmutation of life's substance into a matter of the spirit, but one day, watching the ritual, I thought to myself, "Why, of course! 'This is my body.'"

Food has always been central to religious rites. And the

human ceremonials that join a family by food and wine, or a wife to her husband, are not basically foreign to a tern's offering of a fish to its prospective mate.

I wonder further, whether or not the fish, essential to the existence of a tern, and with which it must feel some primal attachment, is not also a mark of what has to live forever. Symbols indicate that what is being symbolized cannot be utterly consumed. In all this basic ritualizing might be the seeds of human concepts of immortality.

The fish itself is a mystery as well as a reality. I had always seen them as something incomparable. The first spring alewife migrating into fresh water out of the sea, flashing through rocks, was a silver blade packed with energy. I who was also of the living store of earth met it symbolically. I saw it the way I saw first things before an age when I could imagine I knew better. So the terns themselves seemed all youth and no old age.

12

Vulnerability

An unusually early hurricane hit Massachusetts toward the end of June, while I was away in Maine. It was a disaster for the tern colonies in the state. At the ternery off the salt marsh, the loss of eggs and chicks was nearly fifty percent.

I had been through hurricanes on the Cape before. I had experienced the early silence, heavy and dull, and then the distended roaring of the wind, tree limbs cracking and falling, the bay waters seething white, cutting sand riding the air, and salt spray driven inshore for miles. I had thought of those terns on the day of the storm, wondering how they endured, how they acted during it. Perhaps many of them, forced off the ground, were riding it out, beating low across the salt marsh, while others were managing to stay on their nests. Afterward I found that waves had broken over the low, frontal bluff of the island that faced the beach, wiping out the nests there. On the rear levels facing the marsh, the nests were flooded out. Only those on higher ground in the center survived.

While we were in Maine, my son and I had taken out the skiff and traveled between channeled islands to reach a rocky islet where perhaps a hundred pairs of Common Terns had nested the summer before. We landed there—while the birds flew up and hovered overhead—made a quick count of the nests and left. For whatever reason, relatively few chicks scuttled for cover into the scanty vegetation, the rocky nooks and crannies. Many lay dead, some eggs were obviously rotten, others contained dead chicks that had been about to hatch.

Had the chicks died of exposure or starvation? Was the ternery being harassed by gulls? I found it hard to know, though it appeared that most of the adults were not attending to the business of brooding and rearing chicks with much intensity.

A study made by Dr. Ian Nisbet of the Massachusetts Audubon Society shows that in colonies that are doing badly, chicks are fed less often and in smaller quantities, with the predictable result that their growth is poor and they often starve to death.* These weak and neglected chicks are easily killed by predators, and in such a colony their parents do not do much to protect them. Even at the beginning of the season, colonies conspicuously lacking in vigor lay smaller clutches, and often smaller eggs than normal, incubate them less faithfully, and feed their chicks less well after they are hatched. The assumption is that, like the colony at Plymouth, these terns are affected by a poor supply of fish from the start. Since Common Terns feed on whatever kinds of fish may be available to them throughout the season, their failure seems to indicate that in the

---

* "Disaster Year for Terns," *Man and Nature* (Bulletin of the Massachusetts Audubon Society), December 1972.

colonies which are managing badly *all* the acceptable kinds of food must be hard to find.

Dr. Nisbet found, oddly enough, that terns located in Boston Harbor and Buzzards Bay, both of them heavily polluted, were doing far better than in most of the other Massachusetts colonies. Perhaps, at least for the time being, the small fish in these areas were thriving, or, if you wanted to be facetious about it, fatter and easier to catch. In any case, there is no reason to assume that polluted waters will have any but an adverse effect on marine life and therefore terns, either now or in the long run. Not only do they face great hazards in the normal course of their wild lives, but the environment they depend on no longer seems as dependable. They may be able to ride through a hurricane level of sacrifice, but there are other imposed disasters that they hardly deserve.

Having only recently delighted in those noisy, jumping, bombastic chicks farther south, I found the evidence on that Maine island very sad. A dead chick, lying on the sand, or on rocky ground in its nest of scanty humus, grass, or rockweed, is nothing but a pinch of down, a flattened bit of dried fluff with a beak and two legs. Where has all that fierce insistence gone that spoke for the race of terns along the sides of the globe? Immortal eagerness is often pathetically served.

On another islet, twenty minutes to a half an hour away by boat, forty or fifty terns had nested the year before. Johnny Thompson, who ran a lobster pound nearby, told us that after some boys had come out from town in a boat with guns and shot a number of birds, the rest of the colony deserted.

At best, the Common Tern does not compare well with the Roseate or the Sandwich when it comes to successful nesting. Their egg and chick mortality is much higher. Aside from the Roseate Terns' ability to bring in a more consistent supply of fish, without being so dependent on inshore fluctuations, their chicks are well hidden. It takes a practiced eye to find them down in a pile of rocks, and in mid-summer as the vegetation grows thicker, it is very hard to find them there too.

The rate of mortality for Common Tern chicks is very high. Perhaps as many as eighty percent do not survive their first year. Since sea birds are unusually long-lived, however, a population can normally withstand these ravages. An adult pair during a life span of around twelve years might only have to raise two or three birds to adulthood in order to maintain a population. Twelve years is the average, but many individuals live a great deal longer than that. One Common Tern was found to have been banded twenty-five years before, and in Maine in 1970 Ian Nisbet found an Arctic Tern that had been banded as a chick thirty-four years earlier. The annual mortality for adults is thought to be between ten and twelve percent.

Sometimes terns will desert a nesting ground entirely, either as a colony, or, more often, scattered pairs. They tolerate human disturbance on a casual basis, and even those who carry on a regular routine in the middle of them, provided they don't linger too long or hide in a blind. Twice a day, except when it rained, the research staff on Great Gull Island traveled around the island to check on nests, and though they roused the birds temporarily, incubation did not seem to be seriously affected. Most of the birds returned promptly to their nests, as if accustomed to the routine.

Least Terns, which nest on the mainland or on large islands away from the other species, seem able to withstand a lot of disturbance, and are very persistent in the face of losses. Nevertheless, if they and the Common and Roseate Terns are to survive on our shores, their nesting areas will have to be even more carefully protected. Human access has to be strictly limited. The few Arctic Terns that still nest in the crowded Northeast are even more vulnerable, and are doing very badly in spite of conservation efforts.

A dog that runs loose through a colony for any length of time could cause the birds to desert. So could rats, running through a ternery and destroying chicks, in their cold, relentless way. Food shortages might have the same effect, and I am sure there are a number of other causes I have not heard about. The game warden in South Carolina who took me in his boat to see the Royal Terns told me that one colony of Brown Pelicans had been thrown out unintentionally by its protectors, who had put up a *Posted* sign on the shores of their nesting island. It was apparently so large that the Pelicans, and a number of Royal Terns, were greatly disturbed by it and moved out.

The year 1969 was disastrous for the Sooty Terns breeding on the Dry Tortugas. They deserted their nests entirely. At first this was attributed to disturbance as the result of a number of sonic booms coming from military planes flying in the area; but a single, very severe boom was finally thought to be the most likely cause. During the following year, when no such major shock occurred, nesting was again a success, and some 30,000 chicks were raised.

If young are destroyed after the season is well on its way, the birds will not try again; but if their eggs are destroyed, they may renest in the same territory, if not on the exact same spot, or they may desert to another place nearby or a good many miles away.

Obviously, alternate sites are needed—and these days they are becoming hard to find.

It appears that tern populations can survive wholesale destruction of eggs and chicks, or even the loss of generations of adults persecuted by man, so long as it is not protracted. In this country, a serious onslaught against the terns began with the demand for feathers in the millinery trade in the last quarter of the nineteenth century. At one time, there were some enormously abundant tern colonies along the northeast coast. In 1870, as many as 100,000 birds were to be found on a single beach in Nantucket. But at this time the plume hunters were killing 40,000 to 100,000 terns a year, and by the 1880s the terns had been reduced to a fraction of their former numbers. The tern population never did return to what it had been, though in the 1920s and 1930s, after laws protecting them went into effect, they began to make a comeback.

Further attrition is now affecting terns along the North Atlantic coasts, as well as Europe, because of competition from a huge population of Herring and Black-backed Gulls, brought about by the human waste available to them as food. These gulls have been forcing them out of their nesting sites, and sometimes destroying eggs and chicks. A large colony may be able to hold its own. In fact, if the gulls are not too numerous, terns may share nesting grounds with them—the opposite ends of an island, for example—but as the gulls increase in number, the pressure begins to tell. In fact, they are likely to take over the terns' breeding grounds even before they arrive in the spring.

The gulls seem to have been the chief factor in forcing terns off many offshore islands that have historically been more to their liking than inshore territories. They seem to have nested more successfully there than in sites close to the mainland, partly because the shallow seas are richer in marine life.

There seem to have been some recent indications that the gull population might be starting to level off. The filling of dumps, and some curtailment of offshore fishing and its wastes, might in part account for it. For the time being, at least, this was not necessarily hopeful for the terns, simply because hungry gulls would certainly prey more boldly on tern eggs and young. They might also move in closer to shore if less food was available over coastal waters, and compete with the terns even more insistently for their nesting sites. Yet human appropriation of territory along the shoreline may be a greater threat to their future than the gulls.

So the population of terns along the East Coast continued to decline, though a notable exception might be the Roseate, which seemed to be holding its own. Although Roseate Terns had declined in Massachusetts from 5,000 pairs in 1950 to some 2,300 pairs in 1972, they had increased in eastern Long Island (notably on Great Gull Island), bringing the total on the East Coast to between 4,000 and 5,000 pairs. This amounted to possibly 90 percent of all Roseates nesting north of the Caribbean—a precious heritage, if we only knew it.

Arctic Terns in Massachusetts, the southernmost limit of their breeding range, were never very numerous as compared with the other species. They had dwindled by 1972 to about 100 pairs, and there seemed to be little hope for them here. Common Terns, after reaching a peak in Massachusetts of from 30,000 to 40,000 pairs in 1920, had declined to 7,500 pairs, and the Leasts, estimated at 1,500 pairs in 1950, were now down to 950.

I had never really thought of that island, with its beach

fronting on the bay, and the salt marsh behind it, as being anything but a prime site for the terns. I hadn't originally known that it was a second or third choice for them, even though I knew that the natural world had been far richer in the not too distant past. Hundreds of thousands of black caps and immaculate sea-gray feathers once stirred on the islands, appropriate to the long Atlantic shore; untold millions of Passenger Pigeons, appropriate to a great continent, had darkened the sky. There were Heath Hens in abundance, and Peregrines. Ospreys could be seen nesting, or diving for fish, nearly anywhere you looked along the eastern shores, and there were many Bald Eagles. The dimension of those riches has become almost inconceivable to us.

I visited Great Gull Island again toward the end of July. We traveled out by boat from New London, Connecticut, piloted by an old coastal captain who liked to talk about the human condition in a garrulous, old-fashioned way. (Leisurely talk used to be an end in itself; when they had the room and the time.) We passed, in the new age, the *Nautilus*, snub-nosed and shining, a nuclear-powered sub that had successfully traveled under the polar ice, and was designed for even more surpassing achievements, annihilating time and space. We passed ship construction yards and factories, cars droned on the highways, planes, with a dull booming, traveled overhead. The old man pointed to a rowboat with several people in it, no outboard at the stern, coming in on the river. "Well now," said he, "isn't that something. A family out in a boat with nothing but a pair of oars."

The captain knew his own backyard of coastal seas with

a familiarity that has become increasingly rare. He had been out so many times on the water that he knew, even in fog or at night, which island he was headed for, and which point on the island. He claimed to know where the boat was without a compass, if only by the way it felt with relation to the waters around it, the cross currents, the swells, the size and direction of the waves, the feel of the wind. That, it seemed to me, was keeping up pretty well with the terns.

No doubt there are plenty of fishermen and sailors who can find their way through local fogs with instruments, and occasionally without them, but true first-hand acquaintance with the weather, as opposed to empty talk about it, is hard to find.

By this time, I had often seen a single tern flying to its island under the fog, with a fish in its bill. Even though the nesting site was invisible, it seemed to be heading directly toward it. I am not sure terns could do as well *through* the fog, if it was lying close to the surface of the water. I suspect the birds might lose their sense of height and direction, though if they were close enough to the colony they might very well hear it as the sound radiated out.

Navigation was not my expertise; that belonged to the captain and the terns, but I think I had advanced in at least one direction. Now when I saw a tern flying homeward after a fishing expedition to an invisible island I felt a bond with it. I knew what called, as we ourselves moved out over a sea where bell buoys sounded. I heard a chick's frantic begging. I knew now what a fish meant to a tern. I knew what hunger meant to their whole society, and how close the great shifts in the weather were to birds that had to endure hurricane winds, sandstorms that covered eggs or chicks, floods, unusual cold, or days of extreme heat.

The chicks were out there waiting for food, crouched down in a nest, or standing in the open, each one surrounded by the constant crying of its tribe, and I felt I knew them. I had shivered at the whole dark danger to them of reaching the light of day. I sensed their inescapable need, while I followed the parent that answered it. I moved toward what I knew now as a home, however temporary, that answered primary desires for food and shelter, for nurture and growth; and how should men have a true exchange with earth unless they knew it fully as a home?

While the elderly captain was steering the boat from the pilot house just above our heads, I watched occasional petrels flinging their way over the massively running waters of the Sound. The sea was cleansed of an earlier fog and was beginning to lose the direct sunlight late in the afternoon; as the waters rocked quietly they seemed to have an animal light of their own; green-gilled, fish-gray, opalescent. Under surfaces that also shone like a knife, or were as dull as a stone, I sensed a presence, that seemed to ask for some deeper witness from its human visitors. Then there was the landing again, with the crying white bodies of the terns still at their business, gliding and dipping, the island's rightful, original claimants.

At about eight o'clock in the evening, as we walked around the island, some of the terns, instead of attacking, hovered off at a near distance, dark shapes in the waning light, like so many great insects. At this stage in the season, apparently, their responses had begun to change.

Many more of the summer's fledglings were out on the territory, begging, and beating their wings. Others were even making short flights over the water, and still others were showing a tendency to gather together in small groups. The total population had dropped, and at the same time, adults and young from colonies many miles away had apparently begun to stop by. There were also many un-mated birds still courting and pairing up.

Something happened that weekend, out on an island which was fairly remote from human crowds—although boats often passed offshore, and the biggest city in the world lay at the other end of the Sound—to remind me that very little could escape human influence. It was not an obvious event unless you looked for it, or unless it was brought to your attention. Though the waters of the Sound still had a wild shimmer on their throat on a hot day, and an air of foggy deep-sea distance, you could not get away from the fact they they were also among the most heavily polluted waters in the world.

I knew what had happened to the Bald Eagles, the Ospreys, the Brown Pelicans, the Peregrine Falcon, among others, as a result of contaminants in the environment. But perhaps I had been too hopeful about terns, even though I knew perfectly well that since they were fish-eaters, at the apex of a food chain that starts with phytoplankton, they must be vulnerable too.

Already the staff on the island had found birth deform-ities among the chicks, not in great numbers, but enough to cause some apprehension. Some were hatched without any down, or with down on only a part of their bodies. One had four legs, and in another the eyes were abnormally small. Still others had lost their flight feathers as they grew, or had crooked, misshapen, or rudimentary mandibles. Wild birds are occasionally born with twisted bills, but deformities like these had not been seen in the colony prior to 1969. Some thin-shelled eggs were found too: when you see one half-flattened by the bird that is trying to incubate it you realize what a monstrosity it is.

Helen Hays and Robert Riseborough, research ecologists at the University of California, later reported findings relatively high concentrations of polychlorinated biphenyls (PCBs) in the abnormal young terns and in the fish the colony fed on. PCBs are used as insulating fluids in electrical equipment, and are added to paints, plastic, and rubber to make them more durable. They are not the only pollutants in widespread use that might cause defective chicks. These are waste products, brand-new in earth's history, that cannot be recycled and converted into organic material. So we proceed, with a good many protests on behalf of our rights to do so, in the use of such products without knowing how high their concentrations have to be not only to cause widespread damage to a few species we can observe but countless others.

Birth deformities caused by synthetic chemicals are not infectious. They occur randomly and unpredictably, so their implications are not limited to the few terns that are visibly affected. The number of chicks with abnormalities—this year it was only a few out of several thousand—gives no indication of how and where the damage may strike. A chick that is hatched blind or with four legs may have a lower concentration of such chemicals in its tissues than one that appears to be perfectly normal. Because defects occur in such a random way, it is also not known to what degree the pollutants must build up before they become harmful to many individuals rather than just a few.

In Massachusetts the same abnormalities were found in tern chicks from areas considerably less polluted than Long Island Sound. If relatively clean waters produce them too it is clear that the contaminating agencies are extremely widespread and even harder to detect and identify than if they were only localized.

Low hatching rates among tern colonies in the Great Lakes had also begun to show up. The eggs examined showed high concentrations of DDT, dieldrin, and PCBs. Evidently these were above some critical level, since other eggs with lower concentrations had hatched successfully on the East Coast. You might suppose that this sign of an increase of chemical pollutants in the environment would appear in other animals too. In fact, egg-laying snakes seem to have disappeared from southern Texas.

That terns seem relatively resistant to DDT and its derivatives does not appear to have much significance, given technology's ability to develop new contaminants without knowing what their long-range effects may be. We have already put enough into our soil and waters to distort life as we have inherited it. Technology has its own burden of proof; it has to be given the benefit of the doubt when it comes to correcting its own errors. Yet its ability is as nothing in magnitude and complexity compared with a process whose reactions when interfered with may be impossible to predict, and whose outcomes are ultimately unknown.

At Great Gull Island there were three such deformed chicks in 1969; thirty in 1970; nine in 1971; and only four in 1972. Why? Was it because PCBs were beginning to be phased out by industry, or, for some undetected reason, because a particularly virulent combination of waste elements happened to occur in 1970? Those who tried to identify the trouble seemed to be faced with a vast, largely unseen area of cause and effect, and it would take them a long time to pinpoint the dangers to life before they were unleashed. Nature as usual provides the eventual results without necessarily revealing how she got there.

Why should only a handful of malformed chicks be a

matter of much concern? After all, four is nothing as compared with the average mortality of the young. Natural disaster is imminent in all creation, nor are we immune; most of us learn that or are compelled to. One has to recognize, at the same time, that the human race is an incurable gambler, partly defying and denying its losses by creating a sort of separation of power between it and non-human life, to its own advantage. We know we are not guaranteed complete immunity from natural process, but we invent it just the same. Yet, when all is said and done, the harm inflicted on these chicks meant an extra burden we had added to chance. It risked the earth's capacity not only to nurture terns but men.

When I first looked at one of those wretched, deformed chicks, it was not the same as looking at a circus freak, a random product of genetics. We were responsible. We could not afford to say, "Who cares. It's expendable."

Its distortion was a threat to the body of the world, out of whose wild and deep intensity all things were called together. We could no longer play games with isolation.

13

Merciless Renewal

When I came back to the marsh on Cape Cod, I found there were many less young than there should have been, because of the hurricane. Even so, many adults had re-nested and were brooding eggs, but the prospects were none too good that even a minority of these nests could produce young that were able to migrate in the fall.

In any given season, nesting should be finished for the majority by June 15, and some of the young will have fledged and begun flying by July 10. By mid-August, activity is about over and the terns starting to flock away. Since the call of the community is stronger in them late in the summer than the need for individuals to go on rearing their young, chicks not fledged by that time are deserted, left behind—a stark fact that needs to be thought of in context.

How short life is—but how short the year in its constantly varied but scrupulous exercises! The summer days poured by, backing and filling like the clouds and the waves. The duration of the light changed consistently, but it was hard to catch the time, as it disappeared like the wake behind a ship. If there was an eternal moment perhaps these sea birds caught it, diving like arrows to meet their needs, shifting in their motions with the shifts in the tides and in the atmosphere. On the nesting grounds, out over the water stroking buoyantly, dipping with limber ease, they followed a theme of merciless renewal.

Even in early August, summer was beginning to merge with the roving season. An outwardness was growing in their feelings, an inevitable change. The island would have to be left behind fairly soon, though they took its memory and location with them thousands of miles away.

Many of the young I watched were already dividing their time between begging on the ground and making sporadic flights. Just how accomplished they were depended a good deal on their age. At three to four weeks they could fly short distances, and at about nine weeks they could fish for themselves, though some of the more precocious could do it earlier still. Even so, I was to see many young birds begging from their parents well into the fall.

The little ones kept flapping their wings as they developed. At first they just shook their stumps, but with the growth of feathers and wing muscles they would also jump and dance while they fanned the air. It was a joy to see a nearly fledged chick, eagerly facing its breast toward the sea, and beating its wings in such a hearty way, on the brink of achievement. They were called "Orvilles" on Great Gull Island. They *asked* you to cheer them on. First flights occasionally ended in a tumble on the ground, or a crash landing over the water, which meant they would have to swim back. But they kept at it indefatigably, day after day, flying a few yards at first, then farther and farther, until they managed to take off and land again with a fair degree of skill.

While they were hopping and spreading their wings against the wind, they also showed signs, even on the ground, of feeding for themselves. Now and then a chick, newly feathered or nearly so, would pick up a bit of thatch or seaweed and toy with it a little, and I saw one make a futile scurry in the direction of a moth as it flew past.

While I watched those minor acts, I really felt elated at times to think how ordinary discovery had to be to satisfy me. Once I sighted an adult Common Tern eating a brown and orange butterfly. The insect's wings fell off as the bird ate its body, and I felt I had made a great find for the day.

Their first spontaneous flights over the water were unexpected, perhaps because they were arrived at so gradually. Unless you are able to spend all your time watching a colony, the stages of transition can only be guessed at. Finally I saw a few young birds making brief swoops offshore, picking up bits of debris and dropping them again. They were not accompanied by their parents, so I supposed their activity came under the heading of self-learning.

As more chicks got to the flying stage, they seemed more randomly distributed on the ternery, some bunched together, others at various distances from their original nesting places. A parent would occasionally spend some time flying over, calling for a chick, and when its chattering cry came in answer, the adult would sweep down to feed it, even if it was with a number of other hungry juveniles.

There seemed to be a natural teasing involved in getting

a chick to feed for itself. An adult would fly down and stand next to a six- or seven-week-old chick that was begging violently as usual, but without a fish; and the young one would poke in a futile way at the parent's empty bill. Once I watched a young bird wait for its parents for an hour and a half, and when one of them finally showed up with no fish and then started to leave again, it pattered off too as if it was about to fly, though it failed to. Occasionally a fledgling would fly up briefly after an adult who was apparently a stranger, as it cruised over in a leisurely way with a fish in its bill.

A fish that was too big for a nearly grown chick to manage—or perhaps it wasn't hungry enough—was brought in by a parent and left lying on the sand. At first the parent bird had poked at the fish as if to persuade its offspring to eat, but the chick seemed uninterested, so the adult took the fish in its bill again and flew out over the sea. The chick now lifted up and followed, only to see its parent drop the food into the water in an unconcerned manner, losing it for both of them. The young bird made a few shallow swoops toward the surface as if it was attempting to fish, but since it did not seem to be hungry, I had to put all this down to play and practice in the art.

This continued exercise in flying and fishing was probably encouraged too by the fact that a seven-week-old chick no longer had to scurry for cover when attacked, but could lift up into the air. So when a parent or stranger suddenly gave it a peck, off it flew again. Individual adults at this stage, well on in the summer, were beginning to be less intense about going after fish, and could not meet their youngs' demands as frequently. In any case, the withholding of fish had the effect of making the young less bound to the ground where they had waited and begged for food, and being able to chase after their parents in the air now strengthened their skills too.

Although the adults led the young out to fly, they did not appear to teach them how to fish. They did not accompany them during their early fishing efforts. So it seemed that the art of fishing was as much provoked as it was learned by example or imitation. The chicks were partly agitated into practicing their inborn skills, and of course consistent hunger, not only that declared by the gut but also the inner drive which ran them back and forth from nesting and feeding places as they grew, and finally out over the water, played its role.

To see a chick achieve the moment of flight is to realize that the practice of growth is unfailing. They seemed called ahead, I felt in them a pull of distance that was perfectly timed.

A certain number of quite young chicks, two or three weeks under flying age, were still being fed so late in the season that I was a little afraid for their future. The high flights of courtship could still be seen too. Fish were being withheld and offered on the ground or carried in flight—ceremonies that could not be completed except as another year allowed it.

Militancy was still in the air. Once I saw a female grab at a fish that her male companion held in his bill as he pattered and circled before her. Then there was a tug of war, which according to behavioral theory is not exactly a lovers' quarrel, or even an outbreak of domestic anarchy, but the struggle of contrary impulses.

Half-grown or almost fully-grown chicks engaged in

tugs of war over fish too, and this sometimes occurred between Roseate and Common Terns that were being fed in the same vicinity. The young were always highly enthusiastic about running out and snatching what they could get, "rightfully" or otherwise. Usually a parent hesitated before landing to feed its young if there were many other chicks in the area. Running interference from other adults to begin with, as they swooped down to give fish to their own brood, they were often met by other hungry young rushing forward at the same time. If the fish was not instantaneously grabbed and swallowed, someone else not in the family might pick it up off the ground, and might even try to take it away from one with a fish head already disappearing down its gullet.

It is rare to see a tern carrying more than one fish at a time but this did occur on the Farne Islands now and then, and on Great Gull Island an observer saw a Common Tern bring nine small fish at once to its chicks. They spared no time as the fish splattered over the rocks in front of them, rushing around in a near frenzy, picking them up and gulping them down.

During the nesting season, and perhaps to some degree throughout the year, these birds that act so gracefully in unison never lose the chance to take from one another, to be on top. In some ways, begging and screaming, they act like would-be dominant protesters, continually riding those nearest to them. Why, come to think of it, should I run down my neighbors for doing the same thing?

Stay long enough with terns and your head is filled with their foreign cries, and you find yourself listening, sometimes in irritation, to a non-human wildness intent on its own ends. They waste no effort on inwardness and reflection. They never seem to stop working and battling to sort out their mutual actions, to follow an equilibrium. For a man with a hankering for harmony, it might all sound like mere nagging, but this constant begging and quarreling is a partner with earth's great hunger, and in that we could recognize ourselves.

Have I not met terns most intimately in a well of dreams? My unconscious never leaves me alone with my attempts to approach others, to steal my chances. Both birds and men are involved in constant inner relocations. I think that the underwater cosmos which contains all minds, or the rudiments of a mind, must seek to coalesce, to relate, and combine, without final injury to everything distinct and original in the nature of being.

Certain patterns repeat themselves in the life of terns, as they do in men. A chick begging ardently for food from its parents reminds you of a female during courtship. Its rapidly repeated "Ki-ki-ki-ki-ki" is much the same sound, though harsher, less musical, as a female makes with head lowered when a male is pattering around in front of her with a fish in his bill. She begs, half resistant to being led away, half tempted to grab the fish from him. He offers and at the same time withholds. Both are constrained. Their rituals are as formal as their need, at all stages of growth.

Begging in the young got louder and more insistent as they grew older. A chick might even beg from a recently fledged bird as it flew over, though it would stop if the other landed nearby. The begging of the young sometimes sounded determined enough to be calling anything within earshot, or even the sky itself. But since parents and young knew one another, and a parent was reluctant to feed any chick other than its own, the chick usually got its food from that original source—with the exception, of course, of what it stole.

More hunger begets increased aggressiveness. When food is short, growing chicks will attack others when they see them being fed with even greater passion than they ordinarily show. During bad times, the result is that many chicks may starve.

I saw in chicks a violently concentrated and primitive desire, a great impatience that implied a later capacity to be skillful, to seize the moment. In their begging, I saw that all life must fly like the light for its fulfillment, against the will of time, the fact of attrition. We know this in ourselves. Certainly those small birds do not have the great dichotomies of humor and lack of it, of hate and love, of joy and despair, that a man has in him and often lacks the strength to hold together. Still, their inner world, stripped of that human capacity, starts with the same profound demands. In their behavior, they too are reconcilers of opposites. There is a sustained fusion required of both of us to live and beget life. Conscious control does not bypass original need. The rituals we both pursue were not invented by one race and unconscious in the other.

To beg is everything. An often tragic wanting is the most binding sense we have. I beg, therefore I am, the weight of earth, and even that escape from earth which makes men envious of space, inside me.

On that centrifugal territory, to which the terns had come and which they were soon to leave, chicks still hopped and screeched. The adults still postured, with gestures that were half defiant, half appeasing. I could see one hunger in both. And in them all was the turning of the globe against the sun. An outwardness, a great call to move on was changing them. They went on acting out their

needs—begging, fishing, feeding young—but they also began to gather together more, bathing together and fishing
in small flocks along the shore. There were markedly fewer
birds on the island. Many had already left, either because
their young were fledged or because their nesting had been
a failure.

The nearly fledged young were not gray and white like
an adult but had an overall tawny look, bits of down
wisping up between their smooth, clean feathers. They still
begged with chattering, machine-gun rapidity, but they
were beginning to take off and hunt food for themselves,
scanning the waters in the manner of their tribe. They had
short tails, and their wings were not fully developed, so
that at first they dipped awkwardly over the surface of the
water. They lacked poise, and they had to work hard
against even a moderate wind. There was a clumsy aimless-
ness about their flying. Also they tired easily and soon
settled back on the ground. But they went on growing in
skills that had great distances to measure.

After a hot afternoon that had followed fog and rain and
southeast winds the day before, the skies changed again as
it grew darker, with upward-sweeping clouds moving fast
overhead. Most of the terns had settled down, but I
watched a pair in a high flight, up where the weather was,
as they flew together, overlapping, swaying, and swinging
back and forth, passing over and under each other, slipping
gradually past a saffron sun whose eye blinked through
spreading clouds—it was an easy, loping interchange that
lowered down like the light itself toward the sea.

14

The End of a Season

By about the middle of August, there were no more terns flying over beach grasses and sandy hollows when I came to look. For a while longer I saw numbers along their island waterfront, begging and preening, or cruising back with fish; and miles away from there I found groups, large and small, resting on sandbars or flying far out over the flats at low tide. Many of these probably came from colonies other than the one in the marsh, since terns do not migrate southward immediately after they leave their nesting places, but begin by flying over feeding grounds that may be many miles distant in one or another direction. Roseates that bred in Long Island Sound have been sighted during the month of September all the way from there to Cape Cod, the Gulf of Maine, and Nova Scotia. Commons may be seen locally in the fall from Nova Scotia to the Carolinas. They range widely for weeks, until by November most of them will have left the northeast coast for good, and have migrated to Central and South America. A few

Common Terns have been sighted along New England shores as late as December.

Colonies are not fixed as to size and numbers. There is a considerable interchange of populations along the coast. So the birds themselves, having a kind of shifting variety in their motions, obliged to use a marine world that is itself consistent but changing, do not all migrate at once. They move out in flocks of varying size and meet others to fish.

The young that set off for the South Atlantic, never having been there before, must get more practice or direction from their migration than they derive from a few weeks of plunging awkwardly for fish off New England shores. They must still be learners and followers certainly.

Those that still stayed on the ground, chittering loudly, demanding attention from their parents, were well feathered out, but you had to assume that family ties for a good many of them must hold for quite a while. If Royal Terns fed their young on migration for seven months, how long was it for a Common? The assumption was that it was for a much shorter period of time, but it seemed likely that at least some of the young went on being led to fish, and fed intermittently, until it was no longer needed. You get the strong impression that some adults are much better parents than others, and would go on feeding the young longer. Many parents are simply incompetent. They wander off and stop feeding their young before they are able to feed for themselves. Much of the high mortality among young terns in their first year must be the natural result.

It also seemed likely that a tern's ability to find its way might derive from directions it took from the stars, or from the position of the sun, as well as from recognizable landmarks along the way. For the young, following a parent, or flocking with adults that had taken the same route before, might also help in learning the way. This would not apply to young Sooty Terns taking off across the sea for Africa unaccompanied by adults; but species of birds differ greatly from one another in their patterns of migration. I certainly could not envision migration any longer, as I had once thought I could, just by looking at a map. The great passage of wings through the atmosphere asked for much more than that. A profound global learning must be involved to achieve consistent journeys over thousands of miles, across millenniums, and if learning is too human a term then I have to marvel at affinities which seem beyond our conscious ability to dissect. There are endings to which we never come. The earth is a place of passage that is never completed, whether the participants are minnows moving from the mouth of an estuary to a salt marsh creek, or Hudsonian Godwits flying, as they do on migration, at an altitude of 20,000 feet between Hudson's Bay and Argentina. We are inclined to talk of the extraordinary synchronization this life travel involves as if it were fixed, locked in, but since we ourselves depend on it most profoundly, perhaps our concepts need enlarging.

Now I came to the rhythms of a departure I could not follow. The movement of the terns became one of dispersal, and at the same time, unity. Whole flocks acted together, fishing, resting, flying off sandbars when the tide rose. They moved along our shores like small clouds running before the wind.

I never saw actual outflights in large numbers from the Cape Cod colony late in the season. I only gradually became aware of the birds' disappearance from the island. But I did have outflights described to me as they occurred at Great Gull Island in August and September. Apparently these flights started when a local bird flew up, and attracted more and more to follow, until in silence thousands, often diving low over the water at first, streamed out to sea. When they returned, rising slowly together and then descending, there was an unusually loud outcry on the island.

J. M. Cullen has written of evening flights made by Arctic Terns, in which as many as forty or fifty would ascend into the air until they reached an altitude of several hundred feet. Then they would begin to fly off on one course, only to shift to a second and even to a third, as if they had not yet decided on any particular direction. They moved with steady wingbeats, disappearing, passing off overhead and then coming back into view, their feathers glinting against the sun. Were these flights another expression of unresolved feelings that only needed something to set them off?

Such flights seemed to have started with a panic, after which a few birds kept on rising high together and displaying instead of returning to the ground. As a group rose higher and higher, the displaying birds dropped out and alighted, while the remaining ones changed their pattern of flight, flying up, heads into the wind, their wings beating steadily. They were not bunched as in a panic, but flew loosely together and somewhat apart, though clearly oriented to one another at the same time. As I understand what has been observed, these birds might return again to the ground, or they might continue moving into the distance as migrants. They would include both young and adults, and apparently such flights occurred only during the evening. It has been suggested that there might be a correlation between the height at which the Arctic Terns set off on migration and the time of day—another of those fascinating speculations that touch on the many formalities through which the terns carry on their lives.

There is a quixotic quality in the life of terns that is hard to assess. It is like seeing a wild dancing on the surface of the water that has no apparent cause. You can be fully aware of their responsiveness toward one another. You can feel the shifts in their motion as being appropriate to the moment. You can even define specific actions. But what really stimulates them is often undefinable. Perhaps this is only a way of naming a depth of the psyche. What is it in a tern? An impossible question. But either you say, "That is all they know and what they are limited to," or you recognize some inescapable kinship in which earth directions are profoundly involved.

On Cape Cod at the beginning of September, between the tip of North Beach and Monomoy Island, I watched crowds of Common Terns as they fished for schools stirred up by tides racing through the cut. The birds hit the water in such numbers that they sounded like so many paddlewheels. The crowd whirled as one entity while individuals pitched down out of it, fluttered up, and dove again.

As they fished their wings beat tirelessly and steadily, with tails flexing and spreading apart. Occasionally one would change position in the air, halting as it hovered with a shuddering in its body. Beyond the wild, intensely concentrated flock, others chased each other, making grating, excited cries, beating ahead in dipping, striding flight, lifting from side to side.

On some days I could also see a fishing boat a mile or so offshore carrying a vibrant, crying cloud of terns behind it. John Cole, editor of the Maine *Times*, recently described a day's fishing for bluefish when he was a boy:

. . . an afternoon surrounded by swirling masses of snow-white birds who screamed without letup. It was a sound of frenzy, bordering on hysteria, and it fitted perfectly the exhausted, confused and heart pounding mood of the boys on that boat who had never before known the utter excitement of bluefishing.

Surely the experience was one of the keys to my life's later decision to give up every expected career and become a fulltime fisherman. As that fisherman, I came to know terns as friends and providers; they could find fish better than any man or machine, and a person who learned to understand tern language would be told where the fish might be found, if indeed there were any to be had.

I have seen, several times, more than ten thousand pounds of fish in a net because they were located and targeted by a single tern; and I have heard terns talking across miles and miles of water about schools of fish I could not see, but which the terns could sense and find.

While I watched the Common Terns racing back and forth, or dropping down out of a canopy of wings, I caught sight of a Least Tern alighting on the sandy beach beyond, and then one or two more fishing along the shoreline. These were survivors of an environment that seemed to be even less favorable to them than to terns of other species, whose nests were less dispersed and so could be delimited and fenced off. The population of Leasts had begun to decline seriously, all the way south to Florida, and the principal cause seemed to be the overwhelming human encroachment on their nesting places. Along the East Coast there was hardly a few hundred yards of sandy or gravelly beach left where they might have nested successfully.

Beaches and dunes everywhere were bordered by "second homes," high-rise apartments, motels, gas stations, shopping complexes, parking lots, restaurants and bars, cut up with groins and jetties. Beach buggies tore along the beaches or across the dunes, trash barrels were emptied on them, and people by the millions spilled over them all summer long.

In 1972 Mrs. Erma J. Fisk of South Orleans, Massachusetts, counted only 1,400 Least Terns in 2,000 miles, by checking every beach along the Atlantic coast that could be reached by car. Only two years before, she had counted that many in a single area in New Jersey.

Least Terns are adaptable to human disturbance to some extent. They have been found nesting on spoil banks along a highway, and in one instance they even used the gravelly roof of a Florida supermarket. Better conserved, they might raise twice as many young, since they are more persistent than the other species, but our habits seem to be loading the scales against them.

The Leasts are wonderfully intense little birds, with a brightness of being that never seems to tire. John James Audubon said of them: "Nothing can exceed the lightness of the flight of this bird, which seems to me to be among the water-fowls, the analogue of the Humming Bird. They move with great swiftness at times, at others they balance themselves like hawks . . . then they dart with the velocity of thought to procure the tiny fry beneath the surface."

When fishing, the few I saw off Monomoy Point gave a call of "Week-week" and as one of them landed, lifting its wings momentarily in a V, it gave a short, rapid "Chipee." If any behavior can be musical, the Least Terns' is. Hearing their silvery, tinkling cries, the chittering tremolo as they flew over, I have found it pointless to translate the sounds into "Tilik," "Wuhtuk," "Tika-tika," or whatever

I thought I heard. Their cries sounded as if they had continuous edges, links, and vibrations in them that made a singing language, communicating their every act.

They flew up, winging fast; they dove into the water, flew up again to hang fluttering, then dropped like handkerchiefs, little cloaks and bells of the air. There was a fluttering quickness in them, a readiness in every move.

I had seen them in Maine, in Europe, off New England, and on one trip south during another spring, always in small numbers. I came closest to them along the banks of a causeway in northwestern Florida, which passed over an inlet and gave access to marshes and a beach. The ground where the Least Terns were starting to nest was made of bits of shell, gravel, and sand, covered with a scanty growth of grasses. There they had made some very small, bare scrapes. A few pairs had laid their one or two immaculately clean little eggs, which matched their surroundings to perfection. I had to first spot the birds as they flew down, to sit gently in the open light, before I could discover where the nests were.

I remember how very hot it was in early afternoon, when I started to leave the place. I drove the car slowly along the causeway, passing within a few feet of one of the birds as it sat on its nest. Its wings were spread slightly apart, and its bill was open, panting in the heat. As I parked and leaned out the window for a closer look, it moved its head nervously from side to side. It became more than just a field note, throbbing there before me, apprehensive and excitable. How could my own pulse fail to respond? There is a burning commitment in us without a name.

A day later, at a beach in Louisiana, I spent an hour or so watching Black Terns. They had an easy drifting flight, perfectly fitted to sweep between reeds and grasses in marshy ground, where they caught insects. During their migration in late summer from inland breeding grounds to coastal areas, these marsh terns also eat shrimp or fish. At certain latitudes off South America and West Africa during the winter months, there is said to be a continuous merry-go-round of Black Terns picking up food out of the surface of the sea. Where I watched them, they were sweeping and dipping toward the water, making a number of passes, but then taking their food with the kind of casual skill that makes you say, watching a champion performer, "It looks so simple!" They have an impeccable breeding plumage, with black heads and underparts, and back and wings of a deep gray. They seem to be more silent than their black-capped relatives. They give a light, shrill "Keteek" or "Kik-kik" on the wing.

There were Black Skimmers along the shore too; they rose with a wheeling surge into the air, then dipped and cruised on sinuous wings low over the surface of the water, plowing it lightly with those curious, long mandibles that snap shut on small fish after they stir it up. There was a wonderfully supple beat to their long, thin-edged wings. When they stood in the shallows I noticed that some dipped up water with their bills to use it when preening. Since it was spring, one pair exchanged a few ceremonious bows and then stood apart, composed, facing a light wind, holding their proboscis-like bills forward. I could hear a slight "Uhk-uhk" as if they were quietly musing or humming to themselves. When disturbed, they flew off with a cry of "Ahnk-ahnk," like horns at a New Year's party.

Flight in terns was an adventuring. Among their kind, there seemed to be no end of ways to twist and soar and heel in the air, to synchronize with the wings of others. This swinging excitement in early May, these dives and passes, were ongoing in act and form, moving through spring fury and its variations, into a summer that only seemed to linger, into inevitable migration.

So these earth carriers went on tirelessly flying, following the needs of generation. Along the shores of the Cape, the adults flocked and dove where fish were plentiful, and where they were less so one tern carrying a single silver fish would draw a crowd of others after it, crying in high excitement. Sometimes I watched an almost loose, floating motion in them that would change furiously to a wing-fast, shooting forward in flight. The birds dipped and wheeled, they cast themselves into the surface, and all through the autumn I looked for their sickle wings and their sinewy beat along with the slow soaring of gulls and the quick flight of plovers or sanderlings. Hundreds of shore birds were piping and trilling in the distance at low tide, and the "Kleep-keahlee" of Black-bellied Plovers, the "Keearrh" of terns, and the baying of Black-backed Gulls marked their movements from one place to another.

The tidal changes, the channels, and the sweeping of low waters over sand went with their motions, conspired with sea-diving wings. The young ones, begging, fishing, learning control, wariness, avoidance instinctively, as we ourselves may learn them consciously, had an inbuilt obligation to being sent ahead. There was a distance toward which they grew.

Many of these juveniles still fished without tangible results, making incomplete dives, dipping into the surface again and again. Miles from their original nesting places, they roosted along a beach, on offshore rocks or buoys, or even on the rim of a dory as it rocked on its moorings. They could be seen using the same roosts day after day. Some would fly up from time to time when a parent flew over. I saw two young Common Terns flying after an adult, begging harshly, until it dove and came up with a fish which it presented to one of them in the air. With a couple of upward lunges, the young bird swallowed the silver food in flight, like a man gulping something down while he is in a hurry to leave.

Through continual practice, and with the greater assurance that came to them as they grew a little older, beating upwind, maneuvering back and forth, they became more successful at fishing. Where fry were heavily concentrated, flashing at the surface of a cove or the mouth of a tidal creek, or far out over the flats where channel waters ran by a sandbar, they could pick them up more easily. So I could understand again how fine a balance there was between skill and scarcity.

As September progressed, the young flew in a much more effortless way than when they had been making short and awkward flights over the territory. Their wings had a sure beat, though they lacked quite the pliant control they would acquire later on. Their cries were no longer the harsh, repetitive tones of a begging chick. By October or earlier the voice of a young Common Tern changes from a dry, high-pitched, squeaky sound to something like the "Keearr" of an adult, a sort of trilling, short "Keer."

On October 9, I saw a flock of six or seven hundred terns fishing at the mouth of an estuary, the kind of place where small fish congregate heavily in the autumn. By this time most of the adults had molted their summer plumage, so that they had white foreheads like immature birds, and it was hard to tell one from the other at a distance, though the young were still gray and buffy colored, they had docked tails, and they lacked the red beak and legs of a breeding adult.

One day, off on a long, thin sandbar that showed up clearly in blue waters bobbing with small waves, I saw a twinkling line of terns, which began to break up as the tide rose. With them were some larger gulls which stayed on as the waters rose and the bar began to disappear, while the terns gradually fluttered up and separated, until all of them were finally beating low across the water along the shore.

Again, on a windy day in October, I saw one of those lithe, buoyant wind-runners wheel down and land next to its mate—or perhaps the two were unmated birds still courting. The bird on the sands stretched neck and head and the flyer dropped its wing slightly; so a recognition was repeated, a bond retained.

On November 1, I counted forty or fifty terns over the tidal flats at low water. In the ensuing days, I counted a few more, but there were no more big flocks anywhere on the horizon. A few birds were reported during a Thanksgiving storm, slowly flying upwind just off the beach, and I was told of three or four terns in Provincetown Harbor as late as December. None were to be seen after that.

In a colder season, those harsh, expostulatory cries with their ratchet-like vibrations were lost to my ears. The ancient landscape of the tides, with its side-winding ripples between ribs of sand, its wandering pools and runnels streaked and lighted by sun and wind, shifted inexorably, while the terns flew down the coasts and over open seas. The practiced reach—in need and in growth—which I had seen in them since they arrived in May seemed as relentlessly impelled as it was full of grace. The great exercise of life, of which their tribe was such a persistent example, made terrible demands. The clouds were suspended in a sky as gray as northern stone, and I suddenly felt the extreme testing of all things. Having faced a season of terns, what man, or what society, could afford congratulations?

15

Rare as a Tern

That thin line of sand and beach grass between tidewater and salt marsh was left whistling to itself again. In September I had found a few dry corpses of adult terns. The scrapes the colony had made could be seen for a long time after that; but wind and rain were beginning to erase them, and one storm pushed in waves over the head of the beach, carrying wide swathes of sand that buried plants and grasses across the territory. The island looked even more tenuous now, a precarious place for bringing up life, but as central to it as any other.

Their breeding season is for the terns the most dangerous and exacting time of year. As a matter of fact, the fall migration is relatively easy by comparison. Migratory flocks move over the seas at a leisurely pace. Individuals, spaced fairly widely apart, unless they find concentrated schools of fish, fly loosely and flexibly over the water, diving and fishing as they go. Perhaps the Arctic Terns have more to contend with on their world journeys, but most of the terns that leave our shores are having the equivalent of a vacation. They take their time, feeding as they go, resting from what is, after all, a supreme effort.

Aware of the incredible drive they had shown over a period of scarcely three months, a man could nevertheless be excused for doubting that it was possible for a tern to succeed. How could they manage on their narrow margin between life and death, bone and feather by survival! I found myself thinking of the survivors as a living achievement, a tribute to the race of terns. What could equal them? What miraculous entities they were, full of such fierce tenacity! They were rapt of eye. They were superb in flight, and their senses were highly tuned. As their wings skimmed on the wind, I might pray for some fitting perception in myself.

It was true that they were driven, and dependent on the mercy of chance, or on some equalizing principle in forces over which they had no control, though I do not suppose that is unfamiliar to us. Like the rest of life with which we can only sympathize, only receive, because we have its examples in ourselves, they had their common problems and harassments. They were a quarrelsome race. Some individuals were less capable than others. Some lost their lives, or the lives of their young, because they were incompetent. Others, equipped though they might be to avoid disaster, only ran into it head on. And mortality, among those violently eager chicks, was the rule as much as the exception. All this belonged to nature, and no amount of human attempts to cancel the odds, or get rid of inconvenience, could deny a life need that was basically defined by risk. Coming in on them as I did, from the outside, from a human construction and view of things that demanded protection in an often extreme and exclusive way, I had learned something about terns that I had not known before. They had helped me jump my limits.

So the terns had departed. They come again; I never expect to catch up with them. Their image flashes on my mind, sharp and graceful, and I wonder where they are, how the water looks beneath them, where they are headed for. What did I miss? Did I interpret their actions correctly? It is a bird of the round world, unfinished in spite of us. I need more years in which to follow them, not just as an observer but for the sake of our mutual life. I need more play, more extension, more wings.

I am writing this half way into another season in the following year. The story is full of natural calamity again, along with enough successes, here and there, to give us hope. In Massachusetts, the Plymouth colony, already weakened by a lack of fish in previous years, and hit disastrously by the hurricane of 1972, was completely abandoned. Their numbers had already dwindled from 1,500 pair before the hurricane to 400 pair, and in this season they were preyed upon by a large population of rats that persisted in spite of all efforts to eradicate them.

A new colony of Least Terns, near Morris Island in Chatham, with 120 nests, had its chicks destroyed by a pair of kestrels bringing them back as food to their own young.

The island off the marsh had twenty-five percent of its chicks eaten by Great Horned Owls early in the season, before they finally left it alone. After several weeks of fog and rain, the weather suddenly cleared during the second week in July and there were several days of intense heat, with the thermometer reading 92° and 94° in the shade, with offshore waters often calm and free of wind. Such heat on open sand is murderous for an exposed chick. Large numbers died, but these were young hatched in June, half grown and no longer being brooded. The very young chicks still covered by their parents survived. These adults flew back and forth between their nests and the water, wetting their feathers so as to cool their chicks, an action that can only be described in terms of a pure devotion, the kind that stands up to all calamity.

When I visited the Maine islet again in July, there were perhaps a third as many adults to be seen as in the year before, plus a number of nests that had obviously been abandoned. I found the head of one adult, which I supposed meant that this little colony had been raided by an owl. There were only four young, a few weeks old, to be seen, though they seemed perfectly alert and ready to take on the world. I could only wish them well. The rarity I could now see in them struck me deeply.

Rock and sand; water and wind; shining grasses; the cry of new life and its sudden death. In these islands the Great Horned Owl, the kestrel, the Black-backed and Herring Gulls, were bound together with the terns. Is it outrageous that an owl or a hawk would kill so many chicks? I suppose it depends on where your sympathies lie. But in our world, with its great range of choice but uncertainty as to ends, it may be best not to come out too hard for one side against the other. From within the natural economy, I suspect, the common exchanges between life and death exclude moral judgment. If there is an unfair and unnatural imbalance, we might be partly responsible for it, in any case. Since men were a major factor in forcing local tern populations inshore to less favored nesting sites, they exposed them to greater predation.

There is a marked division between the nesting island off the marsh and the peopled shores and mainland behind it. Both nests and houses are temporary. In our age that is more true than ever. Men and terns live in the same world of shifts and changes, less predictable for us than we would like to think; but the nest building and swapping on our part is getting to be chaotic. The terns are far more orderly, despite their behavior. What we call use of the environment lacks a knowledge of its subject which is inherent in a tern. Our relation to territory is strictly on a cash, and therefore wholly abstract, basis. We neutralize it; we eradicate its distinctions. No tern could do that and survive. What life can the earth have if it is treated like used merchandise?

Still, when I go down toward the sand dunes and the open water again, the great distances are still there with an old freedom and reality of their own. They seem to be saying: "You are only half alive to what you need. Space is not exhausted. Desire is infinite; and earth's detail forever incomplete." The appropriateness of a tern, and of its nesting site, is not only a matter of immediate ecology, but the result of great exchanges, meetings between living things and their cosmic community which are lost in time. It is the kind of alliance we cannot afford to do without. We will not be able to manage it alone without this congress of wind and water and sand, and its underlying attachments and messages, sparked and set off in countless unseen ways.

What does this common planetary existence mean but a depth of alliances? There is more to terns than regimentation and recurrent habit. Their repeated rituals and migrations, their passionate, seasonal needs, are part of a world search and discovery. They are active in the dynamic interchange of things. Their life represents a very high order. Do they not have to be as flexible, as responsive, as circulatory, as the waters of the sea?

I think now of the fish carrier, offering the vital symbol to its prospective mate. Have I not felt myself offering and withholding, with some deep wanting in me, some undefined end? Perhaps I was trying to keep my earth feelings on course. How can we know all the mysteries that send us on? Human achievement deceives us. We have to go beneath it so as to admit the unknown.

The realm of survival as I saw it in terns often seemed pitiless, and at the same time it was subtle, binding, regenerative. It gave as much as it took away. The principle in natural life is association—starve that and all foundations are weakened. As the tide moves out beyond my window, I hear a tern cry out again, head and bill bent down, scanning the water for its running food. That it lives, that the fish live, that the tidal currents distribute nourishment for the teeming world offshore, depends on a collaboration that is as exalted as it is matter of fact. The terns teased me into reaching after them, and I suspect there is no end of that for any species. Life is an aspiration that will not exclude. Where else should we go for our directions? Hasn't the earth been calling us for a million years?